RICH BROTT

Biblical Principles for

Staying Out of Debt

7 Things You Must Know!

Published by
ABC Book Publishing

AbcBookPublishing.com
Printed in U.S.A.

Biblical Principles for Staying Out of Debt:
7 Things You Must Know!

10 Digit ISBN: 1-60185-009-3
13 Digit ISBN (EAN): 978-1-60185-009-6

First Edition, January 2008
Richard A. Brott

About the Author

Rich Brott holds a Bachelor of Science degree in Business and Economics and a Master of Business Administration.

Rich has served in an executive position with some very successful businesses. He has functioned on the board of directors for churches, businesses, and charities and served on a college advisory board.

He has authored over twenty books:

- *5 Simple Keys to Financial Freedom*
- *10 Life-Changing Attitudes That Will Make You a Financial Success*
- *15 Biblical Responsibilities Leading to Financial Wisdom*
- *30 Biblical Principles for Managing Your Money*
- *35 Keys to Financial Independence*
- *A Biblical Perspective On Tithing & Giving*
- *Basic Principles for Maximizing Your Personal Cash Flow*
- *Basic Principles of Conservative Investing*
- *Biblical Principles for Becoming Debt Free*
- *Biblical Principles for Building a Successful Business*
- *Biblical Principles for Financial Success – Student Workbook*
- *Biblical Principles for Financial Success – Teacher Workbook*
- *Biblical Principles for Personal Evangelism (out of print)*
- *Biblical Principles for Releasing Financial Provision*
- *Biblical Principles for Staying Out of Debt*
- *Biblical Principles for Success in Personal Finance*
- *Biblical Principles That Create Success Through Productivity*
- *Business, Occupations, Professions & Vocations in the Bible*
- *Family Finance Handbook*
- *Family Finance Student Workbook*
- *Family Finance Teacher Workbook*
- *Public Relations for the Local Church (out of print)*

Rich Brott and his wife, Karen, have been married for 35 years. He resides in Portland, Oregon, with his wife, three children, son-in-law and granddaughter.

Dedication

This book is dedicated to each of my incredible children, son-in-law, and granddaughter and to my wonderful nieces and nephews. How fun it has been to gather at family reunions and spend time with each of them. Below you will find their names listed by family.

Rich Brott Family
Ollie & Julie White
Ella Faith White (granddaughter)
Jana Brott
Nathaniel Brott

Daniel Brott Family
Rachelle Brott
Makayla Brott
Taylor Brott
Ethan Brott

David Brott Family
Andrew Brott
Michelle Anthony
Lisa Brott
Jonathan Brott

Dan Koenig Family
Cara Hall
Nathan Koenig

Jeff Neihart Family
Sarah Zeleny
Carrie Knaebel
Valen Neihart

Mark Powell Family
Jeremy Powell
Zachary Powell
Katrina Powell

Table of Contents

Biblical Principles for Staying Out of Debt:
7 Things You Must Know!

Introduction

There is a great danger that all of us will make bad financial decisions. It's not that we deliberately set out to do so, we just follow cultural norms and wind up deep in debt.

While many are able to recognize bad spending habits and somber patterns and actively take corrective measures, getting out of debt just brings you to the starting line. Next comes a tenacious determination to stay out of debt. After that follows a commitment to building long-term financial security and independence.

The content of this book will help you to understand seven biblical principles for staying out of debt. It starts out with how to have right thinking and knowing exactly where your money is going. The book ends with teaching you how to set financial goals and how to invest for your future.

To Successfully Staying Out of Debt!

Rich Brott

Principle 1

The Principle of Right Thinking

"There is a way that seems right to a man,
but in the end it leads to death."

Proverbs 14:12

Debt is a burden, a weight, a concern, a worry, and comes with a certain amount of uneasiness. The burden of coping with a large amount of debt is strenuous. Coping with debt-related problems is no picnic. The stress of carrying debt crosses over from your business life, to your personal life, to your marriage and family life to your spiritual life, as well as to your personal health. All the various challenges in each of these areas become greater and more intense when you add in the debt factor.

If you are self-employed or own your own business, carrying a personal debt burden becomes a major distraction from other areas that need your undivided attention. Even if you are employed by someone else, if you are constantly worrying about debt, you are not performing your job to your fullest potential. Without looking closely into your financial history, I can say confidently that to rise above your burden of debt, you will have to reduce and eliminate the plaguing debt. When it comes to debt, you slide into it and slowly climb back out. Benjamin Franklin is quoted as saying, "Rather to go to bed supperless than to rise in debt." Debt puts your personal living in jeopardy and makes your spiritual discipline defenseless.

Right Financial Thinking Takes an Attitude Adjustment

ATTITUDE isn't simply a state of mind; it is also a reflection of what we value. Attitude is more than just saying I can stay out of debt; it is believing you can.

Attitude requires believing before seeing, because seeing is based on circumstances, believing is based on faith.

We have total ownership of our attitudes. No one else has the power to alter our attitudes without our permission. Our attitude allows us to become more powerful than money, to rise above our failures, and accept others for who they are, and what they say.

Attitude is more important than giftedness and is the forerunner of all skills needed for happiness and success. Our attitudes can be used to build us up or put us down—the choice is ours.

Attitude also gives us the wisdom to know that we can't change events of the past: our dumb financial mistakes, our indebtedness, etc. I am convinced that life is 10% what happens to me, and 90% how I respond to it—and with this state of mind, I remain in charge of my attitude.

Attitude is a choice! We have the power to choose our responses to any situation. Two kinds of choice-point filters have a profound impact on our responses: those within and those outside of our control.

Some choice influences, such as gender and age, are outside our control. Others, such as values and education, are within our control. Through our attitude, we can empower the elements within our control while minimizing the effect of those outside our control. We can choose to stay out of debt! That is within our control.

Whether within or outside our control, our attitude can greatly influence our response to the circumstances of life. Do financial setbacks come our way? Of course. Do they have to keep us down? Certainly not!

Your attitude is one of the few things in life you can control. Although you can't foresee financial ups and downs you'll experience, you can control your spending habits now.

Personal Debt and My Earning Ability

A survey on Monster.com asked the question, "How much does your personal debt affect the amount you earn?" Out of a total of 1,522 responses, the answers were broken down as follows:

1. **8%** It doesn't: *I can save as much of my paycheck as I want.*
2. **10%** Enough: *but it doesn't hinder my savings.*
3. **40%** A lot: *The amount I earn makes it hard to save.*
4. **41%** Far too much: *I can barely meet my bills—never mind trying to save anything.*

Numbers released by the Federal Reserve indicate that personal debt (credit cards, auto loans, consumer debt, etc.) exceeds $1.6 trillion. Businesses continue to write down and write off unpaid consumer debt. Bankruptcies are on the rise. More alarming is the fact that more and more of a person's paycheck is being used to pay off debt. Wage earners are devoting an all-time high of over 15% of their take-home pay toward paying down debt. Unfortunately, the good times rarely last. We live in a cyclical economy where ups and downs are commonplace. When the economy cools and jobs are lost, unemployment rises and debtors find themselves head over heels in debt.

What is causing the steep increase in percentages? Many professionals believe that the good times and the great economy of the past led consumers to feel they were untouchable. Nothing bad could happen to them. Their investments seemed to be unstoppable, and their jobs secure. During the good times of market bullishness and optimism, more consumers took on debt assuming that to pay it off would never be a problem. It is easy for most people to get caught up in the euphoria of good times and to overextend themselves with credit card and revolving credit-line debt.

What happens when personal debt is high and a recession overtakes the economy? Major firms lay off workers, blue collar and white collar alike. Manufacturing companies close assembly plants and unprofitable firms go out of business. Workers remaining employed face cuts in wages and dwindling benefits. Less money in consumer pockets means fewer goods and services are purchased. This leads to more job cuts and higher unemployment. The result becomes an even deeper recession, a continuing bad economy and an ongoing crisis.

Often this scenario presses individuals and families to purchase more things on credit, things they could not afford even before the faltering economy. They spend today's wages AND tomorrow's wages on things they think they need today. Of course, this does not work in the long term because at some point a person simply cannot take on any more debt and has no additional cash flow to service the debt. The burden of personal debt turns difficulty into hardships and hardship into personal crisis.

To cope, individuals often pay only the monthly minimum required on revolving consumer debt. This barely covers more than the interest due, and usually takes 40 or 50 years to pay off. No, that was not a misprint you just read, it really does take that long to pay off credit card debt by making minimum payments, no matter how large or how small the debt may be. Personal debt in working-class families has crippling power over their lives. It becomes a great source of anxiety and stress.

I will attempt to relate the following story about crabs carrying a heavy burden of debt. It goes like this. If you put one crab into a pot, it will climb right out. However, if you put several crabs in a pot at the same time, they will all stay there—not one will climb out. That's because as soon as one crab starts to climb out of the pot, the others grab it and drag it back down. In a sense, debt is like a pot of crabs. When you face a personal obstacle in the area of personal finance and try to climb out, debt pulls you down again. When you try to get out of some personal struggles and wrong habits, the burden of debt pulls at you until you start to slide backward. When trying to improve your marriage and family relationships, it seems that the stress of debt reaches out and pulls you down from your upward climb.

Debt is a heavy weight and must be eliminated. It must be expelled, driven out of your life and banished forever. It creates all kinds of debilitating pressure. It can become unbearable and weaken even the strongest person, strongest marriage, strongest business, strongest relationships and strongest financial planning. When plagued with debt that has become out of control, it is often difficult to see the whole picture of any situation, whether it be spiritual, relational or financial. Often the person carrying this kind of stress is unable to make good decisions, has clouded judgment, reacts instead of acting proactively, and seeks only short-term solutions.

Of course, all these descriptions of debt may be familiar to you. Debt has become close to you. Although you can't exactly call it your friend, you do have an intimate relationship with it. It is on your mind every day and keeps you from enjoying the life you should be living. It has taken over your thought life and taken control of your daily living. You have been forced to spend a great deal of time thinking about it. You devote a great deal of your paycheck to it and it keeps you from being the loving, giving person you should be.

Because of your personal debt, your life is owned by someone else or something else. Your life is not your own. You must work at that job because you need the income. You are not able to spend time in furthering your education or pursuing a career or vocation you would enjoy because you are too busy working at a job you don't like or appreciate because you need money to pay your debt. Should you lose your present job, it would become a financial emergency in your life.

When you become debt free, for the first time perhaps, you will truly own your life. You can make money-related decisions based upon what you want and not on what others want from you. You don't have to think of the creditors first and your family second. The new situation becomes family first, all else after that. When you become debt free, losing a job will be difficult, but not insurmountable. Yes, maybe there will be a short- term dip in your cash flow, but it won't become a financial crisis in your life. You will still be able to exist. You will still have food on the table, a roof over your head and utilities to make your living tolerable. It takes a commitment to right thinking, in order to stay out of debt.

Right Thinkers Understand Basic Principles

Learning these basic principles will help you to stay out of debt.

- Many are blessed with a lot of cash flowing through their hands. Bring a halt to some of the flow.
- Attack the problem aggressively with a plan. Your credit problems didn't just suddenly appear. It took a lot of steps to get into trouble and getting out will mean taking as much time, if not more, to draw up a financial recovery plan.
- Debt is incurred because we want something before we have the money to pay for it.
- Debt is nothing more than borrowing from future income to buy now what we cannot afford with current income.
- Getting out of debt is an attitude before it is an action.
- How do you get out of debt? Just like you got into debt-one small step at a time.
- If money isn't working for you, it's working against you and you just don't know it yet.
- If you are not content where you are, you will not be content where you want to go.
- If you don't borrow money, you can't get into debt.
- It's not what you make, it's what you spend.
- Keep track of every penny. Know where your money is going!
- Make impulse buying difficult. Leave your checkbook and credit cards at home.
- Stop spending more than you make.

- The fear of doing without in the future causes many Christians to rob God's work of the very funds He has provided.
- The only problem with borrowing money is that you have to pay it back.
- The purpose of budgeting is to free you, not confine you.
- We buy things we don't need with money we don't have to impress people we don't like.
- We should avoid debt whenever possible. In this situation, can I avoid debt?
- When you find yourself in a hole, the first thing to do is stop digging.

It takes real focus and commitment to stay out of debt.

Bad Financial Decisions Come From Wrong Thinking

Do you suffer the consequences of bad financial decisions because you have faulty thinking? Do you need to renew your thinking? Life seems busy as we hurry through our hours, days, weeks, months and years. At various seasons of our lives we need to stop and re-assess what we have been doing, where we are now and the direction we are headed.

Proverbs 14:12

> "There is a way that seems right to a man, but in the end it leads to death."

Proverbs 3:5

> "Trust in the LORD with all your heart and lean not on your own understanding."

Proverbs 3:7

> "Do not be wise in your own eyes; fear the LORD and shun evil."

What past financial decisions have you made that affect the way you are now living? Many of those in financial difficulty really don't know how they got into trouble. They just know that all of a sudden they found themselves in financial jeopardy. It is easy to let our decision making be based upon our current surroundings and the circumstances in which we find ourselves. Is your financial future being influenced by your season in life, your current friends and your need to be accepted? If so, this influence can be positive and productive if you have the right influences, or it can be negative and devastating if you are keeping the wrong company.

Our culture often pushes greed, materialism and a mind-set of "you've got to have it all right now." Our judgment and decision making are easily influenced by the commercials we see and hear, by the friendships we keep and by are inability to distinguish our needs from our wants.

Proverbs 23:4 says, "Do not wear yourself out to get rich; have the wisdom to show restraint." We need to be on guard against personal greed that will lead us to want everything we see and cause us to spend all our energies in a futile attempt to have it all. We must restrain ourselves from seeking things even when we have enough money to purchase them. Additionally, we should also restrain ourselves from purchases for which we have no money and have to go into debt to obtain them.

Going into debt for wants certainly suggests that a person needs a renewal of the mind and a change in the thinking process. Debt is potentially enslaving and we should avoid it at all costs. Proverbs 22:7 makes this very clear to us when it says, "The rich rule over the poor, and the borrower is servant to the lender."

Whether we want to admit it or not, we are influenced by the common thinking prevalent in our "get it now" society. Every once in a while, even normally rational people have to step back and review how we are affected by our surroundings.

Do you have a faulty system of input and thinking? Are you influenced by others to make bad financial decisions? We may find that we need to "renew our thinking." In Romans 12:2, the apostle Paul says we are not to conform or go along with the thinking that is prevalent in our world, but we should think differently, or be transformed. He tells us that this is accomplished by renewing our mind; i.e., our patterns of evaluation, our outlook, our wisdom on any matter, our thoughts, our assessment, our thinking, etc.

Romans 12:2 says, "Do not conform any longer to the pattern of this world, but be transformed by the renewing of your mind." The word "transformation" is translated from the same Greek word that also gives us the word "metamorphosis." This word means to change. If we are not to have the same materialistic mind-set that is prevalent in our culture and society today, then we must change our thinking. The changing of our attitudes about matters of personal finance will not come without a renewal of our thinking.

With Right Thinking You Can Make Good Financial Decisions

You cannot tailor-make the situations in life, but you can tailor-make the attitudes to fit those situations. For many people, the income never seems to cover the outflow. This leads to arguments and high family stress. The stress often comes from deciding how much money to spend, what things to spend it on, and when to spend it.

Some of us spend more time reacting to the fact that we have a problem than we do solving the problem—problems are inevitable. Some problems can be anticipated. Some are surprises. The idea that problems occur regularly need never be a surprise.

The good news is that for every problem, there's a solution. Sometimes the solution is immediate. Sometimes, it takes awhile to discover. Sometimes, the solution involves letting go. When you leave your financial problems unsolved, you in essence are leaving them to chance. You need a plan, a budget and action steps or your financial problems will never go away.

Sometimes problems are a warning sign that you are on the wrong track. You can learn to identify which problems are trying to lead you in a new direction and which ones simply ask to be solved.

All of us have definite ideas about how we are doing financially and just what we want our money to do for us. All of us must take those ideas and commit them to a plan, a financial road map, if you will. This financial plan becomes the written answer, the on paper solution to our financial challenges. You can learn to focus on the solution rather than on the problem and maintain a positive attitude toward life. Things work out best for those who make the best of the way things work out.

What kind of financial solutions do you need to find in your life? Do you have excessive debt? Are you facing college bills for yourself or your children? Are you single, but need to save for marriage? Are you planning to purchase a house or are you simply facing the financial challenge of preparing for your long-term future? The way to connect all these dots is through the design of a good financial plan. This plan, like a good road map, shows you exactly your current financial picture, where you are now, where you wish to be in the future, and what steps to take to get you there. It answers the standard questions of how, what, why, when and where.

What is your solution? What is your plan? Let me suggest an uncomplicated beginning plan that sounds so simplistic that it just might work for you. You can condense it all down to just five words. That is: spend less and save more.

Spending less is a simple answer, but it's not so easy to accomplish. Perhaps you have formed bad money management habits that have haunted you for years. Don't you think now would be a good time to break the bands of bondage? You can spend less by eliminating wasteful spending. Do you really need those expensive toys you only use a few times a year? Sometimes the maintenance and insurance alone for SUVs, motorcycles, boats, RVs, guns, wave runners, snowmobiles and other cash-draining hobbies can run into the hundreds, if not thousands of dollars (this amount, of course, is after the initial purchase cost).

Saving more is the financial solution. Of course you cannot save until you eliminate the debt and payments to service your debt. That frees up cash to save more. If you are a consumer with bad spending habits, you are probably adding to your debt load every month. If so, now is the time to rein in your spending and change those bad habits. Change those bad-spending habits into good-savings habits.

When you find solutions to your financial problems, your personal stress level goes way down. When you waste less money, you have more cash to pay down debt. Paying down debt frees your cash to be saved and invested. Your hard-earned dollars won't be spent on frivolous purchases. This means your long hours and work-filled weeks will be used to make your retirement years more comfortable instead of your current days and weeks more stressful. With right thinking you can make good financial decisions and stay out of debt forever.

It Takes Right Thinking to Understand Right Financial Values

Have the priorities in your financial life been influenced by a faulty system of values? Is your spending out of control because principles of integrity are out of alignment in your life?

A key indicator of strength of character is a person's system of values. Values help each of us determine what is important in our lives. Values set our parameters and provide us with directional guideposts. Our core values and set principles help us make our decisions, and determine our responses to what life hands us. Our actions come from our value system.

A value is a mission, a belief and a set of principles upon which to live our lives. Whether or not they are clearly defined or written upon some paper or e-file, we all live our lives based on some set of personal rules and values. Very few notable people have achieved great accomplishments, enjoyed enormous success or distinguished careers without implementing personal values and underpinning their daily lives with certain principles.

What do you value in life? Are having things more important to you than staying out of debt? Is your work more important to you than your family? Are business contacts more important to you than your friends? Is climbing the corporate ladder of success more important to you than enjoying life itself?

Of course we are not talking about a lack of motivation, laziness or failing to work diligently for our employers, but we are referring to the values we hold close and getting our priorities right. Having a good value system does not come without a monetary cost.

Is accumulating vast resources of money so you can live on Easy Street for the rest of your life part of your value system? Is driving the latest car so you can impress your neighbors and friends part of your value system? Does a sense of pride drive you to continuously out-do others? Are you driven to do more, have more, buy more and show more?

In Luke 12:15 Jesus says, "Watch out! Be on your guard against all kinds of greed; a man's life does not consist in the abundance of his possessions."

A sense of self-worth and all the things that are important in life is directly connected to the core values a person possesses. If you are to be at peace with yourself, your family and your God, you need to rest upon an established base of good personal values, and those values need to drive your every thought, action and reaction. Anything less than that will lead to a violation of the real you. This will lead to confusion, discouragement, frustration and depression.

An important personal value that has nothing to do with money, possessions or things is personal integrity. When you lose your personal integrity you have lost one of the great personal values available to every person alike. This value comes at no economic cost. Compromising integrity for social, economic or financial gain is the fast track to an unhappy life.

Another important personal value that has no economic cost to you is to leave your world (globally and locally) a better place for someone else. Whether you leave a room organized and clean for the next person, a project completed competently, a system working efficiently or a life lived righteously as a model for your children and grandchildren, leave something for someone else. George Bernard Shaw said, "Life is no 'brief candle' to me. It is a sort of splendid torch which I have got a hold of for the moment, and I want to make it burn as brightly as possible before handing it on to future generations."

Sometimes we find ourselves in conflict with our chosen core values. If you say you value charity, but rarely give of yourself, your time or your money, you are in conflict with your core values and not living your life to its fullest. If you say you value family life, but never spend any time at home, a conflict is occurring in your life. If you say that you value good health, but you have poor eating habits and you never exercise, another conflict is in progress.

I began with the following two questions. Have the priorities in your financial life been influenced by a faulty system of values? Is your spending out of control because principles of integrity are out of alignment in your life? If you have found your desires and ambitions have centered on accumulating more and more possessions and keeping ahead of your neighbors, then you have been making financial decisions based upon a defective system of values. Cracks have formed in your foundation. The good news is that those cracks can be repaired.

Financially responsible people who discover that improvements in their financial value system are needed make changes and seek changes in the following ways:

- Saying, "I'll do it. Yes, I will stay out of debt."
- Finding an answer for every financial problem.
- By saying, "I can change my spending habits."
- Looking for a way to make it happen.

- Acknowledging, "Why not! Why not stay out of debt!"
- Saying, "It may be difficult, but it's possible."
- By determining, "I can do all things through Christ who strengthens me" (Philippians 4:13).

You can change your faulty financial value system. Instead of valuing things, you can value life. Instead of desiring the latest, the greatest, the best and the rest, you can change yourself and change your life. You can do it with just a bit of encouragement and support. Yes you can stay out of debt.

Principle 2

The Principle of Knowing Where Your Money is Going

"...your wages disappear as though you were putting them in pockets filled with holes!"

Haggai 1:6 [NLT]

Do you know where your money is going? Have you experienced the common dilemma of having money one day, yet finding that it disappears as quickly as it comes your way? Can you account for every dollar that you have spent?

If you are like many people, you'll find that from time to time cash flow seems to come to a screeching halt just before payday. Actually in several cases, it seems to dwindle just after the paycheck arrives. That which was a mighty river on payday, overnight seems to become a dried-up little creek.

Are you anything like that? Do you regularly find yourself in a cash crunch just before payday? Do you find yourself juggling money between savings and checking because you can't maintain an adequate checking account balance? Perhaps you let one bill payment each month slide into next month. Or, even if your bills seem to be under control, you find it impossible to save any money. Sound familiar? If so, welcome to life.

The Bible acknowledges this problem with a great verse from Haggai.

"Look at what's happening to you! You have planted much but harvest little. You eat but are not satisfied. You drink but are still thirsty. You put on clothes but cannot keep warm. Your wages disappear as though you were putting them in pockets filled with holes!" *Haggai 1:5-6*

Know Where Your Money is Going by Tracking That Missing Money

There is only one way to keep track of your income and keep a handle on just where your money is going. You must use that infamous tracking tool called a budget. Without it you have no ability to plan in advance what your expenses will be and in what areas you will spend your cash. Knowing where your money is going will be briefly introduced here, while actual budgeting will be covered in depth later in this chapter.

Everybody needs some kind of system to account for their spending and cash flow. Spending needs to be controlled. But first you'll have to find that missing money—the income that somehow flies out of your grasp. Ultimately, it's not what you earn that gives you financial security, but what you save.

Many are still trying to learn how to live within their means, instead of living above their means. Yet to save more money and spend it wisely, you must first know where your money goes. And that means keeping accurate records.

You may think the records you already keep are evidence enough. Check stubs, receipts and charge account statements do paint the big picture of your rent or mortgage, utilities, car payments, furniture and other major purchases. But the clues you really need are smaller. What about all your pocket money? How were those $50 withdrawals from ATMs spent? And the $45 department store purchases? What about all of the dollars spent at the coffee houses and fast food restaurants? Can you account for each of those dollars? What do these dollars tell you about your spending patterns?

It's a lot easier to tell others how to budget than it is to discipline yourself! Recognize that it's easy to stumble, to make a wrong choice and fall flat on your face in regards to personal discipline. But don't make that the last word! Get up, start over, get some discipline into your life and get back on track! There is always hope if you don't give up. So don't give up!

So what about that pocket money that seems to elude your financial oversight? If you're like many people today, you don't know because you don't accurately keep track of spending. Yet doing so is surprisingly easy. With that accomplished, you'll be able to analyze your spending patterns, solve the case of your missing money and draw up a realistic form for accounting for the missing money.

Let's assume that you are in the minority and you are now completely debt free. No debt, no obligations...freedom at last! But let me tell you that while many have accomplished this feat, and are now seemingly on their way to the good life, let me assure you that this is only just the first step. You must now begin to save, save, and save; invest, invest, and invest. Becoming free of all debt is just the first step. But the key is not to lose your momentum. You want to stay debt free.

It will be impossible for you to stay out of debt without developing a written budget. A written budget helps you plan for your expenses in advance, before your income arrives. By planning in advance and following your predetermined budget, you will not spend money on things not already in your budget.

The most important part of making a budget work is not how the budget is set up. The most important part of the budget process is you! You are the only one who can make it work.

Many people say, "I just don't know where it all goes" or "I just can't seem to make ends meet." Form a habit of writing down your expenses. Keep track of your outgo. It's surprising what you find when you put it all down on paper.

By putting it on paper, you can...

- Review past spending and saving.
- Regularly record all expenses.
- Intelligently explore all expenditures, and their options.
- Control what you spend.
- Project future spending and saving.
- Enjoy including family members in the process.
- Manage your money, rather than allowing it to manage you.

If you want to become wealthy, you have to save and invest. No, not by buying lottery tickets or hoping your ship will finally come in, bringing you the good life. The first step to riches begins with learning how to budget. You can't save or invest until you know both what you spend, and just how much is available for you to set aside in savings. That knowledge comes with a plan and a budget.

Take control of your income and outflow. It can be fun and will certainly be a challenge. Set up a workable budget that every member of the family (if you are married) understands and supports. Your family and/or friends can become a team pulling together for a common goal. That goal may mean sacrificing now to provide for a college education for the children later (if you are a parent). But it will be worth it when you achieve that goal. If you have been in debt more years than you care to remember, you can look forward to the wonderful, amazing feeling you have when you make the last payment on those debts.

Be in control of your financial future. The key to a budget that works is not some sophisticated elaborate budget process—just old-fashioned hard work. You are the single most important key. Take the opportunity to be in control of your money, rather than having your money control you.

Altering a lifestyle isn't easy. But that's what making a budget work usually requires, if you really want to get out and stay out of a rut. If you are tired of being broke all the time; if you are tired of being dissatisfied with your finances; then set up that budget and make it work for you!

Get Started Now

First, categorize and list all regular expenses. This will give you a financial snapshot of where your money is going. Because everyone handles his or her money differently, there isn't one method of categorizing that is exclusively right. Design a system that fits your personality, can be applied consistently and tells you what you need to know. If you're a generalist, don't attempt a detailed system with lots of categories.

On the other hand, if you're a person who likes detail, don't adopt a system that's too general. Use more detailed tracking for those categories that cause you the most problems and stress. Some need to watch their expenditures in the area of sporting goods and tools, while others need to focus on clothing expenditures.

Next, add up your total income and expenses. If your total income exceeds your total expenses, you've just cleared an important hurdle leading toward "no-debt." However, if your expenses exceed your income, analyze each budget category, consider whether something is a desire or a necessity, and reduce your expenses. Pay special attention to those areas that consume much more income than they should. If not controlled, they can lead to financial disaster.

The most common surprise lurks in the "miscellaneous" category, which often becomes a catchall for everything from restaurants to espresso, film to greeting cards. Once monitored, people often discover they're spending $75 a month on lattes and vending machines, or $175 a month for fast-food meals. Beginners in the budgeting process often find that car payments and insurance are sinking them, and they may be better off driving an older car.

Try to analyze your expenses better. Determine what percentage of your net income is spent per month in each category. To calculate that percentage, simply divide each expense by your net income. (Example: If your total housing costs are $1,000 per month and your net income is $3,000 per month, you're spending ... $1,000 / $3,000 = 33% of your income on housing.) Try to keep your housing expense percentage under 25%.

Designing a budget is more than number crunching and statistical analysis. After all, money is just a tool to help you accomplish something you want. As you work through this process, don't allow yourself to get so wrapped up in the numbers and money concerns and forget the big picture—Everything we have is on loan from God, to use to His honor and glory.

Take the opportunity to do a little day-dreaming also. That might include buying your first house or a vacation home, saving for your children's education (if you have dependents), giving to the church or a charity, taking a vacation, paying off a debt or buying a newer car. If you're married, you need to talk this over with your spouse. Regardless of your marital status, ask for God's guidance (Jeremiah 17:7, 8; James 4:10).

So take a little time to ask, listen and dream. Then establish a few short and long-term goals, set priorities, and adjust your budget accordingly. If you're already into deficit spending, ask God's guidance in making cuts as well.

Some Money Tracking Tips

A budget is a powerful method of gaining control, planning, communicating and fulfilling your dreams. At the very least, a budget should allow you to find extra spending money in your paycheck every month. Everyone can successfully reap the benefits of budgeting; just take it step by step. The payoff is big. It is a great life-changing experience to get and maintain control of your finances. The effects permeate every aspect of your life.

If you are new to budgeting, don't overwhelm yourself and categorize your expenses into too many little categories. Start with a few big buckets at first, until you get the rhythm, then fine-tune your budget.

Make this a household activity by involving all members, and make sure there is some fun in it for everyone. If you never go any further than spending some time tracking your expenses for a few weeks, at least do that. The insights you'll gain from paying attention to your habits will go a long way!

- Be patient. Consider the first three months as a test period. You may have to adjust your budgeted amounts in some categories.
- Invest or save any windfall income. At the very least, treat it with care. Example: tax refunds, dividends and bonuses.
- If you have a quarterly, semiannual or annual payment, such as auto licenses, insurance or taxes, calculate how much those cost you on a monthly basis. Then save that amount each month, so when the bill arrives, it doesn't throw your budget into a tailspin.
- Don't forget to pay yourself. If possible, make sure you save something each month that can go toward an investment.
- Don't try to keep track of every penny (nickels and dimes, yes!). It will drive you and everyone else nuts.
- Make impulse buying difficult. Leave your checkbook and credit cards at home.
- Make sure you set aside some money for having fun.
- Have some fun money for each family member.

- Budget for a fun item (vacation, etc.).
- Don't over categorize (too many "expense" categories).
- Use an interest-bearing checking account.
- Make your monthly savings an "expense" item.
- Create an "expense" item to pay off credit card balances.
- Pay off the highest-interest rate cards first.
- Don't use credit cards again until the balance is paid off...then cut the card up.
- After a loan is paid off, keep paying the loan amount to yourself (make a retirement fund, vacation fund, or car fund).
- Reconcile your budget at least once a month when reconciling your checking statement.

Know Where Your Money is Going by Getting Your Spending Right

Tune in to what you are spending! Write it down. Don't make it a guessing game. Most people do not even know how to tell whether they can afford something. Everyone, not just those who feel they are short of money, should use a ledger detailing all cash flow.

Virtually every business uses a system to define the inflow and outgo of their cash and so can you. No matter how much money you think you have, it's a useful exercise to determine where it comes from and where it all should go.

Some financial advisors recommend a rigid approach to spending: a certain percentage of income for housing, so much for food, this much for installment debt and so on. But others take a simpler and more flexible approach, dividing expenses into needs and wants. These figures taken from USA Today show national averages in various spending categories.

22% Housing (including furniture and repairs)

22% Transportation (car, gas and oil, repairs)
15% Food
9% Social Security, pensions
7% Utilities
5% Clothing
5% Entertainment, recreation
4% Medical care
3% Savings
2% Insurance (except car and home)
6% Miscellaneous

Your first priority is to tithe the tenth (10 percent) that belongs to God. Tithe to your local house of worship. This is the place you receive your spiritual care. Next put away 10 percent for savings and investing. Take care of yourself by setting goals, then treating those payments as fixed expenses. After tithing, the first checks you write each month should be to your IRA, 401(k) and college savings plans.

Then come your living expenses. Roughly 70 percent of your money is usually already spoken for by needs such as rent or mortgage, utilities and taxes. Those are pretty much fixed expenses, although you can reduce taxes with proper planning.

Once needs are met, there's about 10 percent left over for debt reduction and other wants and that's where you begin making choices. You can buy new cars or used ones. Food is very discretionary—you can choose to eat very well or just a basic menu. And clothes—you need appropriate clothing for work, but after that there is a lot of leeway. Every type of expense requires similar thinking. For instance, some heavy readers stock up on books and subscriptions, but you can use the library instead and save money.

One category of wants that many people underestimate (or overspend on) is gifts. There are many more occasions to give than just Christmas and birthdays. All those baby showers, Mother's Day presents and graduation gifts can add up. Take a hard look at what you spend on gifts.

Never Give Up

Remember, if your budget doesn't work the first month you try it, don't become discouraged. Developing a realistic budget takes time. Habits change slowly, especially spending habits. It may take six months or more before your budget begins to work well. At times, your resolve will be tested by everything from a clogged sewer line to a broken arm.

Stick with it. Remember, once you have entrusted your finances to God's principles, He will be faithful to provide for your needs. Using a budget is a sign you want to employ God's wisdom in your finances.

As He says in His Word, "By wisdom a house is built, and by understanding it is established" *Proverbs 24:3 [NIV].*

Principle 3

The Principle of Choosing Cash Not Credit

"The borrower is servant to the lender."

Proverbs 22:7

Get in the habit of paying as you go. Paying cash for an item gives a person that sense of confidence and well being, and keeps debts at a lower balance than the previous month. If you do charge a purchase with the intention of paying it off when the bill comes due, keep a written register of your purchase.

Some people owe more than they own. If you find yourself in the financial position of owing more than your assets or having more monthly bills to pay than your income permits, then it is clear that borrowing has gotten out of hand.

If you do not have money to pay when a debt is due, communicate with the creditor to work out a solution with his/her agreement. It is your responsibility to take the initiative. If you are open and honest with the creditor, most will work with you.

Don't wait for your creditors to come to you if you are going to miss a payment or you have run short of cash. Be up front about it and get them on the telephone! Don't wait for collection agencies to call; call them as soon as you realize you can't make a payment on time. Be honest about the situation and what you can afford to pay each month.

Debt is a Disease

Debt is like cancer. At first it is not life-threatening, because it involves only a cell or two. But it never stays tiny. It begins to grow and then it takes over. It becomes the master; you become its slave. Never believe that a little debt, manageable as it may seem, is okay. It is not. Neither is a little cancer.

Cash Means Major Changes

If you plan to stay out of debt, you will need to make major adjustments in both your lifestyle and spending habits. Plastic, including your ATM card, debit cards and credit cards—are all stand-ins for money. They are not the real thing. They are just representatives, and often poor ones, when they represent debt.

Paying With Cash

Paying cash for a purchase is not generally promoted in our society. In many cases, it is outright discouraged. Why pay cash when you can lease the item? Why pay cash when you can enjoy low-interest financing? Why pay cash when you could be building your personal credit rating? Why pay cash when you may need it for something else?

Of course, all these statements about not paying cash are just silly. If you buy into this notion that paying cash is bad, you are buying into a lifetime of debt. You are becoming the debtor while someone else is becoming the creditor or lender. The timeless biblical proverb still remains credible and truthful. According to Proverbs 22:7, "The borrower is servant to the lender." The principle is black and white: there is no room for an alternate interpretation or explanation. You are either a borrower or a lender.

Choosing to Pay With Cash

Let's get serious about choosing to purchase with cash instead of credit. The bottom line is this: when you pay with cash, you will buy less. You will pay less. You will want less. The professionals are quick to point out that consumers purchase one third less when paying with cash.

The flip side is that when you use credit for purchases, you may buy more than you could possibly need or use, pay more for the item, and pay more interest. When you overspend, you not only pay much more, but you also severely retard your ability to save and invest.

All the places that are trying to sell you everything from cars to furniture to plasma TVs, also entice you to sign on the dotted line by offering so-called "free financing," 90 days same as cash, interest-free credit, no payments until..., etc. Often if you will open an account, they promise a gift.

Of course, we've all heard the saying, "there is no free lunch." And so true it is. Nothing in life is free. It all costs you something. You will pay for everything, and sometimes very dearly.

When you are about to be enticed by sales clerks, TV marketing or newspaper advertisements, pause and think it through. Ask yourself what is the real cost of the item if you purchased it via a credit account.

- Is it really something you need or just buying on impulse?
- Exactly why do you want this item?
- Just how much and how long will you really use it.

If you think that you need it, stop and think; *if you had not gone shopping today, would you have even been considering it right now?*

- If you truly do need it, is this the best price?
- If this store is able to offer "interest free" credit, will the next store discount it if you pay cash?

- Can you afford this purchase?
- Does it make good money sense?
- What will happen if you cannot repay the loan?
- Will making this purchase bring you closer to your financial goals?
- Is this really such a good deal?
- If it all seems too good to be true, then perhaps it is.

What Are the Advantages of Paying Cash?

Consider the following list:

- You will be less inclined to think you really need the item.
- You will delay your purchase as long as possible to preserve your cash.
- You won't be the impulse buyer you would be when using credit.
- You will always attempt to purchase at a discount to use less of your cash.
- You won't have to worry about destroying your planned budget.
- You won't have to worry about making payments.
- You will choose your purchases more carefully.
- You will not purchase your wants before your needs.
- You will be at peace and the purchase will seem more satisfying when you pay with cash.
- You will take better care of your purchase when you pay with cash.

Some of you may try to excuse yourself and think cash could be dangerous to use for it could be stolen. Yes, perhaps that is true, but using a debit card, which is drawn against your bank account that has the cash, is safe indeed. A debit card has the same purchase safeguards as any credit card. When using a debit card, the amount of the purchase is automatically deducted from your checking account as if you had written a check.

Purchasing Vehicles

Think about it. If you paid cash for an automobile, would you buy a brand new one with all of the extra bells and whistles, or would you be more inclined to purchase a great used model?

It's a good feeling to use cash to make major purchases. I don't remember when I last purchased a vehicle on credit. It has been too many years ago. Yes, it does keep me from trading vehicles every year, but who needs to drive the biggest and the best all the time? Only those whose egos need to be maintained.

I purchased all three of my vehicles with cash. Because of it I don't have a lot of extra cash laying around, but they were all purchased new without credit. In our family we have two boats, two pickups, and an SUV. Because we all work in different areas of the city, it makes having three separate vehicles a necessity. If the city bus came near our neighborhood, we wouldn't need all three.

It is a great feeling to pay with cash. I was born in the 1950s. Back then, 33% of all vehicles were purchased with cash. My first five cars were purchased with cash. All five were purchased during my high school and college days.

I was raised with the attitude that you did not buy something unless you could afford it. You certainly could not afford it unless you could pay in full before taking a purchase home. If you didn't have the money, you saved for it first. It is much better to fund your dreams instead of servicing your debt.

Staying Out of Debt

How do you refrain from going into debt? How do you stay out of debt? You simply begin to pay cash for all purchases. If you do not have the cash, you walk away.

Using common sense is the best way to stay out of debt. Have the common sense to stop buying on credit and start paying with cash. If you want to freeze the level of your debt, you simply freeze spending.

I took a cyberspace trip to Bankrate.com, used the online calculators and developed the following calculations. If you have credit card debt of just $5,000 at an interest rate of 18%, and make a minimum payment of 2% of the unpaid balance, it will take you more than 46 years to pay it off. During that time, the $5,000 purchase will cost you an additional $13,931.13 in interest. If you took on this debt at age 19, you will have it paid just in time for retirement at age 65. This makes your purchase cost a total of $18,931.13. I hope it was worth it!

As if that doesn't hurt enough, another cost is involved here. It is the "opportunity cost" of what those minimum payments invested at a mere 12% would have brought to you.

Divide the total cost of your purchase ($18,931) by the 553 months it took to pay it in full, and you have an average monthly cost of $34.24. Investing that monthly for the same time period in a tax-free account would earn you at least $933,682.

So it's quite simple. The choice is yours. Do you want to purchase something at age 19 for $5,000, make the minimum payment and have it paid for at retirement? Or would you rather skip that important credit card purchase and have a cool million at retirement with the very same monthly investment?

These simple statistics will be a wake-up call for many. Time can be a curse or a blessing. Which will it be for you?

What Else Do You Really Need?

Let me be very forthright and direct with you. You already have enough. Stop buying more things! You don't need everything. You don't need the latest, the greatest, the biggest, or the best.

Quit watching television commercials. Stop listening to those who are trying their best to convince you that you just have to buy their product. After all, it will help you live a better, more fulfilled, more satisfied life, will keep you in better health, and make everyone else want to be your friend. They don't care a flip about your well being; they just want your money or your credit card.

Now I want to get right in your face and say this. Living below your means is possible. It is just a matter of making different choices; right decisions.

- How much is enough?
- How many things are sufficient?
- Specifically, just how much money do you need to spend on yourself and just how many things do you need to live in this world?
- How many possessions must you accumulate to feed your appetite for having it all?

Are you happy only when you indulge your every whim to spend more money on yourself, or can you actually be happy curbing your craving for more and more. Is it possible to place self-imposed limits on your current lifestyle and restrict your personal spending? Are you spending your cash for need or greed?

Buying On Impulse

When you find your spending is out of control and you cannot resist buying more things for yourself, building up your resistance to impulse buying is a discipline you need immediately.

The traits of godly people are characterized by the spiritual disciplines to which they submit. Whether it be prayer, purity, integrity, humility, diligence, faithfulness and obedience or selflessness, leadership, servant-hood, and financial stewardship. These are all important.

Economic disciplines include time management, wise spending, hard work, financial stewardship and debt restraint.

What is the key to achieving success in all these areas? The key to success is that of personal discipline. Just as successful athletes must practice the daily discipline of exercise, training and hard work, so you must approach your desire to stop spending money on yourself. Often it simply comes down to this: say "no" and have the steadfastness to keep yourself out of temptation's path.

Borrower versus Lender

Let's contrast a real-life scenario of the borrower versus the lender that happens tens of thousands of times every day. A person walks into an auto show room and falls in love with that new car or truck that has everything he ever desired.

The design is superb, the model fits his or her personality, the safety features are comforting, the interior is sleek and the instrument panel comes with satellite navigational features. Not to mention the surround sound, satellite radio and the leather interior. Just sitting behind the wheel makes you feel rich and successful and gives you a sense of well being.

Of course, in reality, if you do not have the cash to pay for it, and you are not already completely debt free, you are headed for financial disaster. At the very least, you are falling for a lifestyle of debt that has been disastrous to many people today.

Current marketing culture paints a glorious picture of the rich and famous as opposed to the down and out. Yet millions have bought into the payment-poor, debt-bondage lifestyle.

Look at the difference between the borrower and the lender in purchasing just one moderately priced vehicle. Given a very common loan repayment schedule of six years, a huge gap occurs between the two situations.

Here are the two choices:

1. making vehicle loan payments
2. taking that very same payment and investing it in the equity market yielding average historic equity returns over the past 40 years.

The real difference is this. The borrower makes the same payment the lender (investor) does for the exact same time period. When the time period is up, the borrower stops making all payments; so does the investor.

At the end of the six years, the borrower has a used vehicle of questionable value. At the end of six years, the person who chooses not to borrow for a new car or truck, but instead invests the exact same payment, has a total sum of $55,741. This is just for the one-time purchase of just one vehicle.

Wait, that's not all. Both persons have made the very same monthly payment. However, the investor (the one who does not borrow) makes no more payments, but continues to let the accumulation of his or her six-year payments grow in the marketplace, gaining return upon compound return at the very same rate.

In just 4 additional years, the lump sum of payments has now turned into $90,082. Add on another 10 years and it becomes $299,081; yet another 10 years and the total is now $992,985. Finally, after another 10 years it has grown to $3,296,826.

Amazing! All the accumulation has come from just six years of monthly payments. The borrower described in Proverbs 22:7 has a used vehicle of questionable value after six years. But with absolutely no additional contributions, look what the wise person of Proverbs 22:7 has accumulated! This is a clear reminder that the Bible really does make a lot of sense.

Why They Want You To Use Credit

Why are you encouraged to use credit instead of paying with cash? Two reasons are clear to me.

1. ***If you pay cash, you are likely to be more careful in your purchase.***
   a. You may not make the purchase at all.
   b. You may delay the purchase until you have enough cash.
   c. You may decide there are other priorities for your cash.
   d. You may press the vendor for a better deal.
   e. If you do not get a substantial discount on the potential purchase, you may just walk away.
2. ***If you pay cash, the dealer, the vendor, the store, etc., will not get more benefit from your purchase by gaining from a financing deal.***
   a. Carrying your financing increases the value of your purchase.
   b. Carrying your financing provides ongoing interest income.
   c. Offering you credit helps push you toward a purchase.
   d. Offering you credit helps you make a quick decision.
   e. Offering "easy credit terms" gets more types of people in the door to make a purchase.
   f. Offering to finance the deal gets you into the store or showroom much quicker.
   g. Offering to loan you the money makes you think about a purchase you would not have previously considered.

You need to know that vendors who are offering you easy financing for your purchase don't do so for YOUR benefit. It is not offered to you because you are so well liked that the store or dealer just wants to make your life a bit easier. Offering to finance your purchase is purely in the self-interest of the vendor.

Cash Benefits

Five reasons to pay cash!

1. Paying cash means making some lifestyle changes and sacrifices, but it will keep you from drowning in a sea of red ink on your journey to financial freedom.
2. Paying cash keeps you focused.
3. Paying cash promotes contentment by adding meaning and value to the things you buy.
4. Paying cash lets you own things, not merely acquire them.
5. Paying cash makes spending difficult and uncomfortable—exactly the way it should be.

Good Debt or Bad Debt?

Many people, even so-called consultants, will tell you that there is "good debt" and "bad debt." Wrong! Please don't buy into the "good debt"/"bad debt" discourse. ALL debt is bad! Yes, at times we are swayed into a purchase because we don't have the cash, but that does not make the debt good!

The only debt that even comes close to making some short-term sense is a home mortgage. If you cannot make the payments on a 15-year mortgage however, you are probably buying too much house. My recommendation is to limit your home mortgage to 15 years and then do everything in your power to shorten that debt period by making extra payments toward your principle balance.

Some go into debt for so-called investment purposes. They are buying second homes, seaside properties, even speculating in commercial development or in the house rental market. This is a volatile place to put your personal finances. Unless you have substantial cash available to cover for an enormous potential loss in income, run away from such so-called investing.

Leasing is Still Debt

Some think that leasing a purchase instead of paying with cash is a good thing. Wrong! As with any traditional debt, lease is still a cash obligation, no matter how you coin the word.

Coming from the corporate world, I can tell you of faulty thinking firsthand. During the boom and subsequent bust of the 90s, a common practice was to make large purchases via leasing contracts. Virtually everything was leased. Fleets of trucks, manufacturing equipment, buildings, and so on were all leased instead of purchased outright.

This produced a couple of scenarios. First, it encouraged buying even when no cash was available. Second, it kept the "corporate debt" off the Statement of Financial Condition, commonly called the balance sheet. Third, many assets owned outright by the company were sold for cash and then leased back from the new owner. This supposedly freed up corporate cash for other things.

I saw great companies with substantial real estate and other corporate assets proceed to sell off the assets, receive the cash, and then watch the cash simply disappear over a short time period. The company was left with long-term leasing debt and a huge burden to bear for many years to come.

The bottom line of the leasing scandals I witnessed was that the greedy corporate executives boosted the value of their corporate parachutes and boosted the value of their personal stock options. They received unprecedented amounts of company bonuses because of their wonderful achievement of improving the corporate financial condition. After many great personal bonuses and benefits, the executives would move on to other companies and new opportunities to do the same all over again.

Corporate Debt

The real sadness of going into corporate debt was that the investors never knew what was happening to the companies in which they had invested their life savings. The leasing debt was never a part of the corporate balance sheet and because of loopholes in the law, the company auditors never disclosed the debt in the financial reports.

If corporate debt is good, than why is one of the most successful companies ever to grace planet Earth completely debt free? If debt is so good and provides so much so-called tax relief, why is the company that produced the richest man in the world debt free?

Of course, I am talking about Microsoft, which has no debt and many, many billions in cash! Not only this company, but also many others are debt free.

Thousands of others like it have chosen to have absolutely no corporate debt. In the Northwest USA where I live, 34 major companies alone have no debt.

Use the information I have just provided to think about paying cash. If you don't have the cash, don't make the purchase! Use the "cash paying" model of these companies to improve your own personal family financial balance sheet. Perhaps you have made some mistakes in the past. Yes, you must now dig yourself out of debt. Your past is important, but not nearly as important to your present as the way you see your future.

So is there really good debt? Not in my opinion. Perhaps, at best, some debt is tolerable for a short time period if you need a roof over your head or a yard for the kids to enjoy. Make a commitment to your future and the future opportunity of your family. Choose now to pay cash.

Warning Signs of Impending Peril

Some of the nicest people have the worst problem handling debt and credit issues, but unfortunately by the time they realize it, it may be too late. Take these warning signs to heart and decide now to conquer debt before it conquers you.

Fortunately, potential debt problems can be spotted before they reach the serious stage. By knowing what danger signals to look for, you can take steps to prevent a problem before it occurs.

Go through the checklist below. If any of these danger signals looks familiar, you may be headed for financial trouble.

- You think of credit as cash, not debt.
- Your debts are greater than your assets.
- You owe more than seven creditors.
- You are an impulsive or compulsive shopper.
- You and your spouse are dishonest with each other about your use of credit.
- You don't know how much your monthly living expenses are or the amount of your total debt.
- Your expected increase in income is already committed to paying off debts.
- You depend on extra income, such as earnings by a second person or overtime by the breadwinner, to help you make ends meet.
- You have less than two months' take-home pay in cash or savings where you can get to it quickly.
- You have to pay back several installment payments that will take more than 12 months to pay off.
- You have more than 15 percent of your take-home pay committed to credit payments other than your home mortgage.
- You get behind in utility or rent payments.

- You have to consolidate several loans into one or reduce monthly payments by extending current loans to pay your debts.
- You cannot afford to pay for regular living expenses or credit payments.
- Creditors are sending overdue notices.
- The portion of your income used to pay debts is rising.
- This month's credit balances are larger than last month's.
- You are usually late paying some of your bills.
- You borrow for items you once bought with cash.
- You don't have enough savings to meet expenses for at least three months.
- You don't know how much installment debt you owe and you are afraid to add it up.
- You have borrowed money from a new source to pay off an older, perhaps even overdue debt.
- You have borrowed money to pay for regular household expenses such as rent, food, clothing, gas or insurance.
- You have reached your credit limits.
- You hurry to the bank on payday to cover checks already written.
- You no longer can contribute to a savings account or have no savings at all.
- You pay bills with money earmarked for other financial obligations.
- You pay minimum amounts or less on your outstanding debt.
- You use a cash advance from one credit card to make payments on others.
- You've applied for more credit cards to increase borrowing.

- You have drawn from savings to pay regular bills.
- Your liquid assets total less than your short-term debt.

If you identified with two or three of these, it's time to do something about it. If at least four of the above statements applied, examine your budget and look for ways to tighten your belt. If you identified with five or more, you are probably headed for financial trouble. If you identified with seven or more, then your financial health is in trouble. You are in financial danger!

Principle 4

The Principle of Breaking Bad Spending Habits

"For a man is a slave to whatever controls him."

2 Peter 2:19 [TLB]

To remain debt free, one must break free from those unproductive spending habits. When you get sick and tired of being strapped financially, then perhaps you will finally do something to change your current behavior.

Break free from those bad spending habits and those no good all-day shopping trips. Now that I have your attention again, know that the Bible does not teach, as some propose, that all debt is wicked and sinful. However, having said that, it does teach how really awful debt is, and how undesirable it really is. Debt should always be a short-term situation and a last resort. Debt was never meant to be a way of life.

Stopping Debt in its Tracks by Breaking Bad Habits

The only way to get out of debt is to stop getting into debt! The only way to stop getting into debt is not to take on more debt. And the only way not to take on more debt is to break free from your long-lived, unproductive, spending habits.

If you do not have the discipline or ability to pay your credit card balance in full each month, you should get rid of it, or them. Cut up the cards, put them in the deep freeze, hide them in the garage, or whatever you need to do to curtail and eliminate unnecessary spending.

Remember, if you are spending more than you are earning, you are going into greater debt. If you keep spending in this fashion, you are headed for a debt burden snowball – once it starts rolling, it's hard to get it under control again. At this point you will be rolling toward sure disaster.

The road to financial independence comes by making hundreds of small prudent decisions over a lifetime, each seemingly insignificant, but collectively making the difference between financial dependence and financial independence.

One way to break free from the spending habit is to look at the credit in terms of total outstanding balances instead of minimum monthly payments. Each month, pay off all new charges on your cards, plus interest and a portion of the previous balance. You'll reduce each month's debt balance below the previous month's. It should get easier as you go.

Credit cards are not an extension of your paycheck. You end up having less money, not more. Never get a cash advance with a credit card. I have had the same Premium Visa card for at least 15 years. The normal interest rate is charged only when they must pay for your purchases. Cash advances are charged to your account immediately when you acquire the monies, and the interest rate on the cash advance is at least 3% higher than the normal rate.

Many checking accounts offer dangerous overdraft features. These accounts make it easy to borrow money by writing checks even without adequate funds in the account. All these "easy credit" methods will get you into debt trouble and keep you there if you don't make up your mind once and for all to break free from your spending habits.

Change is Necessary to Break Bad Habits

Staying out of debt requires change. Make a decision to change your attitude, lifestyle, spending habits and invest in a new you. When your debts are high and your monthly income is not enough to cover the payments, there are ways to solve your debt problem. However, the road to financial recovery takes a total commitment.

When you make a decision to change, it must be firmly rooted in the knowledge of what got you there in the first place. You must know why you work your entire week just to serve a lender. It's really nothing new; the Bible clearly summed up this same situation many years ago. Proverbs 22:7 says, "The rich rule over the poor, and the borrower is servant to the lender."

Easy In—Not So Easy Out

Debt can be presumptuous. You can assume that after borrowing the money, or signing on the dotted line for that large purchase you really could not afford, everything somehow will all work out. The problem is that this presumption is kind of like driving down the freeway the wrong way with your eyes closed. You are hoping you don't get hit by a tractor trailer coming in your direction, and somehow you will avoid a head-on collision, but the reality is you really have your eyes closed. Unpleasant things happen when your head is buried in the sand or your eyes are closed and you are unable to clearly see your way.

Debt also can be a failure to trust God. After all, many biblical references point out that God is a giver, beginning as the giver of life itself. God gave us all of creation. He gave us life. He gave us His life so we could have eternal life. He gives us what we need. He is the ultimate giver. So why do you mistrust what His Word says about meeting your need?

Overcoming Bad Spending Habits

Debt also can be overcome. Will it be easy? Of course not! Will it be difficult? You can count on it! But it can be overcome. It matters not how much debt you currently have, how little income you currently have or what others say about your situation. The bottom line is this: If you want to get free from the burden of your debt and if you want to be free of stress and worry, you absolutely can get there someday.

But it does take courage. It does take commitment. It does take planning. It does take a budget. It will take change and it will take action on your part. Not just action for a day, a week or a month. It will take consistent, continual, reliable, unswerving, unshakable and steadfast personal, hands-on engagement. But it can be done. You can stay out of debt.

You must decide you want to remain without debt forever. Discipline yourself and take the necessary action to begin to pay back your debts, not take on new debt, and have the commitment to stay with the plan until you are truly debt free. Only you can determine if you are willing to make the necessary sacrifices to achieve this goal.

Getting out of debt is like getting through boot camp. It's a lot of hard work and some days you want to quit. But when graduation day arrives, memories of pain and trouble will pale in the light of the pride and accomplishment you will feel. You made it! You didn't quit. Now you must be committed to staying out of debt.

The Starting Point

Like boot camp, getting debt free is not the end; rather, it's the beginning of a whole new adventure. To drop out at graduation and go back to your old way of living would be to turn your back on everything for which you have been preparing. It would be like closing the door on your dreams of financial freedom. It would diminish the importance of what you accomplished. Who would be so foolish as to do the difficult work and then not stick around to enjoy the reward? So get started, get a plan and let's move on it.

Being in Control

Being in control of your finances means a whole lot more than just earning a greater income, having a better job and controlling your money. It means getting a handle on your bad habits. These might be habits of bad thought, wrong decisions, wrong choices and bad spending habits.

What is it that is motivating you to take on more debt? What is driving your desire to spend until you are out of control? 2 Peter 2:19 mentions this, "For a man is a slave to whatever controls him" *(TLB)*.

How we manage our money affects not only our present, but also our future. It affects how we feel about ourselves and how we react to others. Many of us find ourselves with dismal spending habits that need to be broken. The good news is this: regardless of your past, your future is a clean slate.

Recognizing a problem doesn't always bring a solution, but until we recognize that problem, there can be no solution. Many times the difference between your accomplishment and your failure is your attitude. If you have the attitude that you can take control of your finances and you can break bad habits, then I am confident you will.

Your Current Income is Enough

You already have all the income you must have to meet your basic needs of food, shelter, and so on. It is amazing how much money we spend on everyday things. Forget all the unnecessary purchases you make, you can save significant dollars just on housing, food, clothing and transportation costs.

Much of a bad spending habit involves seemingly little and simple insignificant purchases. You burn a lot of unaccounted-for cash. Is it a need or is it a want? If it is possible to live life without it, then it's definitely a want. If it is possible to delay the purchase, it's also probably just a want. You must know the difference between a need and a want.

Knowledge is good, but your choices must reflect that knowledge. If the potential purchase is a want, then don't buy it. Knowing the difference puts you in control.

Maybe you purchase things just to impress your family, friends and neighbors. Don't worry about keeping up with the Jones'. The only reason you should ever buy something is because you need it, not to impress someone else.

Breaking Bad Spending Habits

Old bad habits are always hard to break. New good habits are hard to form. The good news is that you CAN break bad spending habits and you CAN get rid of your debt. With the right information, coaching and self-discipline, you CAN move to a much better life of financial stewardship. If you have good financial stewardship in your life, you will be blessed. You see, the result of good stewardship is ongoing and continuous biblical prosperity.

Staying out of debt and honoring God by becoming a person of financial integrity is pleasing to Him. Thus, we may need to begin with a heart transformation and a change in our approach and attitude about managing what He has entrusted to us.

Remember that we own nothing and that we are nothing more than managers of what God has placed in our hands. If we mess up on the little money we have to manage, I cannot imagine God will want to heap more upon us only to see it disappear through bad spending habits, poor purchasing choices and bad financial stewardship. It is clear that breaking bad spending habits will take some personal discipline. In Proverbs 13:18, we are admonished in this way, "He who ignores discipline comes to poverty and shame, but whoever heeds correction is honored."

Freedom From Spending

Freedom from excessive spending takes personal discipline to be sure, not only the discipline of self-restraint, but also the discipline of a good work ethic, careful time management, wise choices and good decisions.

Breaking free from poor spending habits takes the personal discipline of knowing where you can go and where you should not go, where you spend your time and the wisdom of how to live below your means. This means utilizing resources already available to you before jumping into your car, heading for a shopping area and pulling out the credit card to purchase what you perceive you need. This is an example of a bad spending habit you need to break.

Often we form bad financial habits because we are discontent with what we have. Scripture speaks clearly about our bad spending habits when it tell us in Hebrews 13:5, "Keep your lives free from the love of money and be content with what you have".

The end result of continual spending and bad financial habits can eventually lead to bankruptcy. This is something you NEVER want to do. It is dishonest not to repay your debts, and it will also cause financial havoc and personal pain for many years to come. Last year bankruptcies were at a record high.

Turn Off the Advertisements

Bad spending habits flourish when we fail to turn down the radio during advertisements, turn off the television during commercials, spend our day off visiting shopping malls, new car dealer lots, etc.

Use your free time in productive areas far away from people and places that exist to separate you from your money. Bad spending habits make you spend hundreds or thousands of dollars without really giving much thought to what you are buying.

To stop the process, begin to write down everything you buy for two or three months. Record every nickel, every dime, every cup of coffee and every burger. This simple inconvenient exercise alone will help you to retard your out-of-control spending.

The Power of Contentment

You can break bad spending habits if you will understand all that God has already given to you. If you take the time to appreciate His goodness, you won't always be on the lookout to get something more.

I Timothy 6:6-10 says this, "But godliness with contentment is great gain. For we brought nothing into the world, and we can take nothing out of it. But if we have food and clothing, we will be content with that. People who want to get rich fall into temptation and a trap and into many foolish and harmful desires that plunge men into ruin and destruction. For the love of money is a root of all kinds of evil. Some people, eager for money, have wandered from the faith and pierced themselves with many griefs."

This verse pretty well puts it all into the proper perspective. We have been given so much already – after all, we came into this world with nothing. If we have food, clothing, shelter, family and friends we have all we need.

2 Corinthians 9:8 lets us know God will always be looking out for you: "And God is able to make all grace abound to you, so that in all things at all times, having all that you need, you will abound in every good work."

Change Unproductive Habits

Additional bad habits besides bad spending habits include those which would cause us to be distracted and less efficient and less productive. These habits should also be changed, broken and replaced by good fruitful habits.

William Arthur Ward, who was an American scholar, author, editor, pastor and teacher, said these short, but very profound statements:

> *"Believe while others are doubting.*
> *Plan while others are playing.*
> *Study while others are sleeping.*
> *Decide while others are delaying.*
> *Prepare while others are daydreaming.*
> *Begin while others are procrastinating.*
> *Work while others are wishing.*
> *Save while others are wasting.*
> *Listen while others are talking.*
> *Smile while others are frowning.*
> *Commend while others are criticizing.*
> *Persist while others are quitting."*

Principle 5

The Principle of Living On Less

"...I have learned the secret of being content in any and every situation, whether well fed or hungry, whether living in plenty or in want".

Philippians 4:12

An oft-quoted maxim is "live within your means." That is good beginning advice for those who dive into heavy debt from living beyond their means, but such advice will hardly provide financially over the long haul.

To live a life that is debt free, bondage free and to head happily toward a comfortable retirement requires a different pattern of living. Financially, you must live below your means.

If you have been living above your means, you are already in serious debt and have no hope of staying out of debt unless you quickly change your financial habits. If you have been living within your means, you may be debt free, but you have little or no savings or investments to carry you through your retirement. What you must begin to do is live below your means.

Why is this important? Unless you believe you will be in excellent health to work even to the age of 80 and above in order to provide food for yourself, shelter and the other necessities of life, you need to save and invest for your retirement years. Doing this is not possible if you are living above your means or simply living within your means.

If you spend more than you earn, you have a very serious problem on your hands—the problem is you! Most people do not have an income problem; they have a spending problem. It's not what you make; it's what you spend.

If you have managed to tame the spending tiger within you and are living within your means, you still have further cutbacks to make in your family cash flow. You need to spend below your available income stream. You need to be planning for your retirement. Your government social programs won't provide adequate income for your retirement days—that, will be left up to you. It is your responsibility, not your friends, family's or government's.

Okay, now you understand the necessity of living below your means. What does that really mean? In a nutshell, it simply means you have to spend less money than you earn. It means you do not allow yourself to spend money on things you don't absolutely need or things that just make you happy for a moment or two. It means you save money instead of spend it. It means investing the money that is left over.

The picture of retiring early, gaining wealth and having plenty of money to give to worthy causes is a picture of a happy life. You are the lender, not the debtor. You are the master, not the servant, because you have learned to master yourself. You have learned to discipline your sudden impulses and you have learned the difference between wants and needs. It's not complicated; it's very straightforward. It's living a simpler lifestyle.

The authors of *The Millionaire Next Door*, Thomas Stanley and William Danko, have spent considerable time in researching the lives of the affluent and the wealthy. Their research led them to the following conclusions about how the rich arrived there, and how they continued to stay that way. From their conclusions, they believe the first point is the most important.

- They live below their means.
- They allocate their money, free time and energy to wealth accumulation.

- They prefer achieving financial independence over displaying/flaunting their social status.
- Their parents did not give them free and frequent handouts of money.
- Their children usually become self-sufficient.
- They are skilled in targeting business opportunities.
- They carefully select occupations that complement their skills and talents and that lead to building wealth.

Their studies show that typical millionaires own their own homes but do not live in multi-million dollar homes or drive expensive cars. More often than not, they buy used cars, bargain for other purchases and live simple lives. They do not live extravagant lifestyles. They usually live frugally.

Seldom do inheritances or advanced degrees build fortunes. The wealthy are usually living far below their means and working very hard. Typical millionaires are willing to give up status to instead invest for financial security.

The greatest percentage of millionaires are self-made. They are some of the most efficient and resourceful people around. In many cases their children are unaware of their family's wealth. Instead of living in plush New York garden apartments, Beverly Hills or on the Florida waterfront, much of the time, they just live next door in comfortable neighborhoods.

Many millionaires are ordinary people who work dull jobs. They have learned important truths: nothing is more valuable than working hard, saving large sums of money and living well below your means. They have learned the important lesson of living on a budget, accounting for their expenditures and paying close attention to their investments.

The only way for you to provide for your later years is to live below your means. If you want to have any hope of achieving financial independence you must live far, far below your means. This is not a difficult concept to understand. Although it is very simple, few people do it. Because it is so simple, people tend to discount its effectiveness.

The bottom line is this. There is no free lunch, no schemes by which you can get rich quick, no ship coming your way, no lottery with your name on it, and no alternative to plain, old-fashioned hard work.

In our culture, impulse buying is predominant. In years predating the present easy credit, you would walk into a department store, see an item you would like to purchase, and put a small cash down payment toward it and then pay it off monthly until the item was paid for. Once paid for, you took it home and began to enjoy it.

Many today fear that without the newest cars, latest toys and exotic vacations, they are missing the train. They find out later that by buying these things, they risk being run over by the train—the fast charging, mounting-debt train that's about to steamroll over their lives.

In our culture, credit purchases are the norm. Often, before an item has been paid for, it has been discarded. If you think you must have it all now or you cannot be happy, a paradigm shift must be made in your thinking. In our culture, going in hock up to our eyeballs is the normal thing to do.

Our culture and society is all about promoting credit, spending, debt and a "I can have it now" way of life. Buy now, think it through later. Buy now, worry about payment later. Live for today, let tomorrow's worries come later. Beginning a debt-reduction program almost seems counterculture.

Living above your means creates high stress levels. High stress levels affect your health, your spiritual life, your emotional health, your marriage and your financial life. Living within your means lessens this stress. Living below your means decreases the normal stress of life much more. Living far below your means gives you peace of body, soul and spirit.

You can build a huge nest egg for your later years simply by living below your means. Does it mean driving a car that should be abandoned in a junkyard? Not really. Does it mean eating oatmeal seven days a week and drinking only water? Not really, but perhaps that would help you with your weight-loss goals.

It does mean monitoring your spending, watching your cash and accounting for every penny spent. It means making conscious financial decisions based upon need and stopping your impulse spending. It means waiting 30 to 60 days before purchasing, giving you time to come to your senses.

What are some of the mistakes that families make when managing their finances? Hundreds of wrong choices could be listed, including those that result from making decisions without knowledge or without taking the time to clearly think them through.

Some mistakes are the result of character issues such as wrong values, selfishness, irresponsibility or lack of integrity. Other mistakes simply are the result of hastiness, lack of education or wrong priorities.

People who have a spending habit that has gotten them into trouble need to make a plan, get out of debt and stop spending money they don't have. Then when they are in complete control of their money, they should go ahead and start saving for specific needs or for a home.

But you first need a written plan—a budget. A written plan stands firm whether you're on an emotional roller coaster or an even keel. Your attitude toward spending should be "no debt, no matter what." Following is a list of 10 financial principles penned more than 100 years ago by President Abraham Lincoln. These truths are as trustworthy today as when they were written. Part of the beauty of these remarks is that they are short, to the point and easily understood by anyone.

- You cannot bring about prosperity by discouraging thrift.
- You cannot help small men by tearing down big men.
- You cannot strengthen the weak by weakening the strong.
- You cannot lift the wage earner by pulling down the wage payer.
- You cannot help the poor man by destroying the rich.
- You cannot keep out of trouble by spending more than your income.
- You cannot further the brotherhood of man by inciting class hatred.
- You cannot establish security on borrowed money.
- You cannot build character and courage by taking away men's initiative and independence.
- You cannot help men permanently by doing for them what they could and should do for themselves.

Living on Less Means Doing Without the Non-Essentials

You CAN do WITHOUT these things:

- Restaurants
- Movies
- Manicures
- Gourmet coffee drinks/snacks
- New clothes
- Hobby acquisitions and/or expenses
- Lodging expenses at the beach, mountains or other destinations
- Unnecessary vehicles (all new vehicles)
- Cable TV
- Sports events

Living on Less Means Enjoying Life Without Spending

Most of the real treasures of life can be had without spending a single penny. We all have rich resources available to us without cost.

What is the value of a great friendship or loving relationship? Everyone can extend friendship to some acquaintance. If not, endless opportunities to offer friendship can be found. How many senior citizens are living in care facilities that would love to feel the warmth of a compassionate relationship?

In the past, people lived from birth to the grave enjoying the blessings of life, yet never had to spend real money to enjoy them. Currently, we think that to enjoy life we must have money to spend.

At what monetary cost is our freedom? Our freedom of mobility, worship, independent thinking, etc., may have come at a cost to past generations, but for us we enjoy them without personal financial cost.

At what monetary cost is a walk through the forest, a rest by a rippling stream, a gaze toward a beautiful sunset, staring upward at showers of stars, a warm gentle breeze, a good read from a book of interest, a trip to the park, etc.?

Equally free are enjoying the autumn colors, the white winters, the colorful spring and warm summer nights. What about the endless puffy clouds of white that fill our sky, a glorious sunrise, and the squirrels that run from tree to tree? These are all priceless treasures of life that bring endless hours of enjoyment to us, all without costing us a dime.

Many people think that it takes money to enjoy life and all it has to offer. I am not of that crowd. Life is all about what you have inside, not what you see and accumulate on the outside.

You don't need 25 years of education to take advantage of the opportunities available to you. Watch any immigrant culture and see how industrious and prosperous they can become with some hard work and simple ingenuity.

A story is told about a former prisoner of the Vietnam war. His name is Charlie. Charlie used to give speeches and presentations across the country.

When he first came on the stage, he took a couple of chairs and placed them about two feet apart. As he began to talk he paced back and forth between the two chairs again and again.

Of course, the listeners were a bit puzzled, yet fascinated at the words he was speaking. They watched and listened intently. Back and forth, silently he paced.

At a particular moment in his speech, Charlie then told his audience that for a period of six long years, he paced, just as he was doing now, back and forth, back and forth in his three-foot-wide North Vietnam prison cell.

Then he continued his story. It seems he was shot down by the enemy and was captured wearing only his tattered flight suit. It was all he had with him at the time of the capture. He was placed into a very tiny prison cell with only the clothes on his back. He didn't have much; or did he?

At this point in his presentation, Charlie engaged the audience, attempting to broaden their thinking and help them appreciate all they had at their disposal. He asked the listeners what else he had with him besides his flight suit.

With their input, he then listed other great assets at his disposal more important than his flight suit. Some of them items on his list were as follows:

- his knowledge
- his acquired skills
- his training and experience
- his ability to think
- his courage
- his creativity

- his imagination
- his ability to reason
- his ability to remember

On and on the list grew until the audience suddenly began to understand that ***some of the best things in life are free.***

Some of his best assets were not the clothes on his back or the things in his possession, but rather the intangible strengths that were his.

If each of us were to do a similar exercise, we could count thousands of ways we could enjoy life without spending money.

Living on Less Means Decreasing Your Expenses

If your spending is out of control, it is time for a little austerity. Here are just a few ways you can cut expenses painlessly.

- **Avoid joint obligations** with people who have questionable spending habits—even a spouse. If you incur a joint debt, you're probably liable for it all if the other person defaults.
- **Avoid large rent or house payments.** Obligate yourself only for what you can now afford and increase your mortgage payments only as your income increases. Consider refinancing your house if your payments are unmanageable.
- **Barter your skills** for someone else's skills.
- **Be aware of your spending habits.** Stick to the lessons you have learned about how you got into debt and how you're living to get out of it.
- **Before you purchase** that must-have item, wait six months and think it through again.
- **Bring your lunch to work.** You will save money.

- **Buy used rather than new.** Cars, furniture, computers, stereo equipment, televisions and appliances can all be found at substantial discounts in the want ads and at garage sales and swap meets.
- **Control impulse buying.** Don't impulse buy. When you see something you hadn't planned to buy, don't purchase it on the spot. Go home and think it over. It's unlikely you'll return to the store and buy it.
- **Clip coupons and use them.** Some coupons are worth the clipping effort and others aren't. The most valuable coupons can be identified by one of the following: biggest percentage, largest dollar value or items used at least once a week.
- **Create a realistic budget and stick to it.** This means periodically checking it and readjusting your figures and spending habits.
- **Cut entertainment costs** by renting videos rather than going to movies, eating at cheaper restaurants, eating out less frequently and brown bagging it to work. Order take-out food rather than eating at the restaurant to save on tips and drinks.
- **Develop an awareness** of the difference between your wants and your needs. There is a difference!
- **Eat out less and at home more.** The cost of food at restaurants, especially when you add in the cost of service, really adds up. Both the food and the service are usually better at home anyway.
- **Save food costs.** Buy on sale, clip coupons, buy in bulk.
- **Shop at thrift clothing stores.**
- **Spend less on gifts.** Be creative rather than extravagant with friends and family. Make your gifts: birthday, Christmas, wedding, etc.

- **Stay at home.** And stay out of the malls...you'll save fuel expense.
- **Stop incurring debt.** Cut out unnecessary spending and avoid impulse buying.
- **Visit your local library.** There are many resources available to give you the particulars on frugal and simple living. It's a great place to check out magazines, CDs and DVDs, etc.

Principle 6

The Principle of Setting Financial Goals

"Commit to the LORD whatever you do, and your plans will succeed."

Proverbs 16:3

"Any enterprise is built by wise planning, becomes strong through common sense, and profits wonderfully by keeping abreast of the facts".

Proverbs 24:3-6 [TLB]

Getting out of debt is one thing, but staying out of debt is just as important. Sometimes after a long journey of getting out of debt, it is easy to get sidetracked and begin spending again as a result of your extra cash flow. The money previously needed to become debt free is not available as extra cash.

This is the exact time when you need to take those extra uncommitted funds and put them to use. By setting short and long-term financial goals, you can make this happen for your benefit.

Only a foolish person would begin a long journey without knowing the destination. Have you ever seriously thought about drawing up a plan for your financial life and deliberately mapping out where you want it to take you?

It may be that you have considered some New Year's resolutions to guide you through the coming year. It is said that there are only two things in life that are sure—death and taxes. However, there is an additional one—time flies! The clock is ticking; the present has become the past and the future will soon be the present. You can either be ready for it or wait and let it take you by surprise.

Your financial clock is ticking and before you know it, that which you thought was a long way off will be just around the corner. The bottom line is that you need to be ready.

An important element in establishing your financial goals is to establish or maybe just review your life's purpose. Where do you want to be financially in 5, 10 and 20 years? From there you can clearly define your financial objectives. Yes, you can choose a new set of New Year's resolutions to improve the coming year.

Analyzing My Financial Goals

- What are my financial goals?
- If I had to identify my primary goal, which one would it be?
- By what criteria do I now establish my priorities?
- Is my lifestyle appropriate to my income goals?
- Which of my financial goals will bring the greatest value to my family?
- Which of my goals will bring the greatest value to my community?
- Which of my financial goals will bring the greatest value to my church?
- Which of my goals will bring the greatest value to myself?
- Are my financial goals realistic?
- Can I make the necessary financial provision to accomplish my goals?

- Which of my goals will bring the greatest personal satisfaction?
- Which goals will benefit the greatest number of people?
- Will my financial goals be able to maximize my investment returns, while minimizing the risks to other family members?
- Does each family member share in my goals?
- Since I feel all of my goals are important, how can I make sure that the action plans for one goal do not hinder or conflict with another goal?
- Do my goals match my income?
- Do my financial goals maximize tax shelters?
- Do I have clearly defined financial goals?

Setting New Financial Goals

Setting some new financial goals gives you control. As is the case with most successful people, you've probably focused more on making money than bothering with learning how to manage it. Although you have your attorney, your insurance agent, your banker, your CPA and your broker, you may not have given a lot of thought to a sound financial plan.

Have you strategized in a way that will enable you to reach your financial goals? You need to. Your financial well-being and success will not come by sheer luck and inattention to your goals. In fact, that will guarantee your family economic disaster.

Financial goals are reached by knowing what you want, where you are going, making informed choices and using all appropriated strategies to set out your course.

Setting financial goals takes the control from others and puts the control of your financial future into your hands. It becomes your blueprint that will guide you through the financial peaks and valleys of life.

Without spending limits and preparations for your financial future by setting current goals, you, your dependents and your assets are not adequately protected against the risks of life. This can lead to needless waste of your current resources. Your daily decision making could be controlled by your current desires, not your future needs.

If you do not take control of your financial possessions now, you will likely pay higher income taxes which may have been avoided with a sound financial plan.

Setting Financial Goals Points You In the Right Direction

It helps point you toward specific family goals and gives you leverage over your financial resources.

What do you need your resources to do for you? Without setting proper financial goals, your long-term needs will not be met. Your children won't have a means to get a good education, your spouse will not be prepared in case of your disability or death, and you will be forced to a retirement income of much less than you might need.

Setting Financial Goals Helps You Know Yourself

Financial success begins by knowing yourself. This includes knowing your objectives, determining your investment goals, your lifestyle and the type of investment goals you are comfortable with.

Since your goals and needs are unique to you, making wise investment choices is very important. You will learn about yourself by taking into account your investment objectives, your tolerance for risk, your time horizon, your financial knowledge and your financial health.

Another part of knowing yourself is setting realistic expectations. Are you one who can accept higher risk for higher potential returns? Conversely, will you be satisfied with lower returns by choosing conservative investments?

The best way to get to know yourself and start down the path to achieving your financial goals is to get time on your side. This can only be maximized if you begin at once.

Setting financial goals keeps you on track.

Living in a busy world with all sorts of demands and opportunities to spend can play havoc with our available financial resources. We all have some sort of money challenges from time to time. It's part of life and living.

This is why setting financial goals is so important. How can you possibly think about the future that is 10, 20 and 30 years out there, when your checkbook is now empty and you won't get paid for another 10 days!

By setting financial goals, when attempts are made to rob you of your cash, you can make the appropriate decisions based upon your previously written goals. Your money will actually seem to go further if you know where it goes.

You must know what you want to accomplish with your income. Know what is wise spending and where you are spending foolishly, and carefully plan your spending in advance.

Taking the time to carefully plan for your financial future is the act of accepting personal responsibility for it. Certainly, there will be times when you need information and advice from outside sources, but the ultimate decisions are yours. By staying on track with your financial goals, you will increase your ability to get what you want out of life.

Setting Financial Goals Helps You To Build Financial Assets

Whatever your choice of investment vehicle, without a goal, you are likely to just hit and miss. Your last choice for spending available income is going to be socking it away for your retirement. This means that whatever is left at the end of the week is what you will save.

Your savings will not grow unless you make it your first choice of what to do with each paycheck. A definite spending goal will help you build assets. You can begin to build assets by first limiting the taxes you are currently paying.

The goal of every taxpayer should be to pay your fair share and to pay everything that is legally owed. Tax evasion is both illegal and immoral. Tax avoidance through proper planning is both legal and moral.

Setting Financial Goals Helps You Prepare for Retirement

Many uncertainties surround the subject of retirement. These include the uncertainty of your health, the economy, inflation, your age, the success of your investments and more. Because of this, it is of vital importance that you start when you are young before time becomes your enemy.

Even if you are ready to retire, setting financial goals is still important. We are living longer than ever before and the uncertainty of inflation and other expenses should cause us to commit to careful planning and strategic goals. When investing, it is important to take a long-term view, giving your investments time to grow.

Setting Financial Goals Helps With Educational Expenses

In building your overall family asset base, discuss with your family what goals they might have in mind. Of course for the parents, this would include retirement plans. For the children, it would definitely include their education.

One of the greatest gifts parents can give their children is a good education. Instead of funneling large sums of money for furniture or a vehicle, let them earn their own money, but give them a head start in their earning potential by helping them get a solid education. This will cut their umbilical cord to your purse strings, enabling them to gain earning power themselves.

Every family must spend according to their family values. This is how they should set their financial goals. It is not that values are right or wrong, rather that values vary from family to family.

There could be the purchase of a new house, a new business start-up in your future or an infinite list of other possibilities. Building assets for additional, yet unknown projects, requires that you continue to set and consider future financial goals beginning now.

Setting Financial Goals Prepares You for the Unexpected

One general goal is to help you protect yourself against a number of risks. These might include the loss of income, the death of a family member, medical expenses, disability, unemployment, property and liability losses and others. At the very least, goals help you set up an emergency fund to act as a buffer for unplanned expenses.

Change is a way of life. Things happen. Life isn't always very smooth. Jobs are lost. Health problems confront. Vehicles break down. Emergencies arise.

Most experts recommend setting aside anywhere from six months' to a year's salary in liquid assets, such as CD's or money market accounts. In addition, it is important to purchase disability income, life, long-term care and other types of insurance to help protect you, your family and your assets against the loss of income, illness, disability or other financial circumstances.

When you recognize the possibility of mishaps that will impact your finances, you can plan for their occurrence in advance. You may have to make slight changes or adjustments in your financial goals, but should something unforeseen come your way, the financial burden can be lessened. Your advance planning can lessen your anxiety and reduce the impact of a potentially severe blow to your finances.

Setting Financial Goals Improves Family Communication

Setting financial goals, launching those goals and staying on track is a family team effort. Setting goals is full of tough choices.

People who do not have a lot of extra income will have to prioritize their spending and separate their needs from their wants and desires. They may not get the house of their dreams, a new car every couple of years or an education for their children at the best private colleges available. Families have to be willing to accept trade-offs.

The entire family must come together to build a sure financial base. If one family member controls spending and promotes saving and the others do not, you will only reach a small portion of the assets you are attempting to build.

Each family member should contribute to setting the goals, determining the priorities and considering the various consequences of not staying with the goals. By working together, it becomes a family project which enhances unity, creates stable relationships, and provides a method to keep each family member on track.

Steps To Financial Goal Setting

To be successful at anything necessitates knowledge of goal setting, measuring progress, and achieving milestones. In its simplest form, goal setting includes the following steps.

Write Down Your Financial Goals

Use paper and pen or your computer to crystallize your thinking. Writing them down leads to commitment. You become open to new ideas about what you really want to accomplish. This helps you prepare and ready yourself for the future. Writing out your ideas helps you to recognize when new opportunities arise.

Gather all of the information that you have related to your current financial condition as well as your assessment of where you are and where you want to be. Then, begin to gather all of the necessary paperwork.

You will need to know exactly where your income is coming from and what your spending habits are. Be very detailed. You must know about your employee benefits, insurance benefits, any insurance policies that you have purchased, your living will, a complete and detailed statement of your net worth, a personal income and expense statement, the likely cost of your child's future education, your retirement desires and, in short, a written document of your past, present and future.

This will take some time, but you cannot prepare written financial goals without some intimate knowledge of your family situation. Have you analyzed your history of spending? Have you examined your spending habits? Have you investigated all future costs? Do you know where your financial leaks are coming from? Have you found the holes in your budget and identified areas requiring immediate change?

Know your purpose, your objectives and your specific goals. If your objective is to be financially sound, what specific goals will you set out for your future to obtain? Define very clearly what those goals are.

- Where are you going?
- Where do you want to be?
- How will you get there?
- Which financial goals are for next month and which ones are for five years from now?
- What are your priorities?

Give Yourself A Deadline

Specify a time for achieving your objective. Get started on your financial journey by being deadline motivated. Deadlines help get you started and keep you moving. You become a person on a mission. You have placed a target in your sights and know where it is you are aiming your life. Goals are worthless without a plan of action and some deadlines.

Develop specific deadlines that will keep you on track toward meeting that goal. In the beginning, you will need to set up a family budget. Consider having automatic payroll deductions for savings or retirement purposes, a plan for contributing to your employer's 401(k) program, contributing to your own IRA account and so on. Look at those specific deadlines, prioritize them and then put them into action.

Financial goals and objectives should cover all time elements. They should anticipate changing needs as your life changes. It is never too early to understand your purpose, lay out those objectives in a clear, concise manner and then set the appropriate goals that will put you on your path to financial freedom.

Set Your Standards High

In general, the higher you set your goal, the more effort you will have to expend toward reaching it. The loftier the goal, the more motivated you will be to reach it. As you reach certain milestones in your blueprint of progress, you'll become inspired to give it all you've got to reach your desired result.

It may seem strange, but it often takes just as much effort, energy and hard work to reach small goals that lead to little more than poverty and misery as it does to reach higher goals that lead to success, prosperity and abundance. So aim high! If you shoot for the moon and miss it, at least you'll be among the stars.

Set Realistic, Obtainable Goals

While it is important to set your goals high, rather than low, you nevertheless must set goals that are reasonable and realistic. In order words, set high goals that will cause you to focus more, goals that require some real pro-active energy on your part, yet be careful to stay within the range of possibility.

With diligent motivation and hard work on your part, perhaps even at great personal sacrifice, high goals can be achieved. Of course a lot of the results will depend solely on the kind of effort you are willing to make.

However, be sure to be level-headed and pragmatic when setting your financial goals. Do not fool yourself or others with any of this pie-in-the-sky stuff. Goals that are set too high so that they become unattainable will be a source of never-ending frustration for you and your family members. While they might look very good on paper, if you cannot reach them, you may eventually abandon all goals and simply give up.

Be Detailed And Specific

Explicit objectives and precise family financial goals must be set. Goals that are vague might never be met. Don't ballpark your numbers or your goals. Don't say to your family, "Let's buy a small farm in the valley in a few years." Or to your spouse, "Let's set a goal of moving to Mexico when we retire." While serving in a third world country might be your purpose and retiring in Mexico might be your objective, when it comes to setting goals, the numbers must be very clear. Numbers would include your age, the year, the dollars needed and every other detail that might enter into this picture.

Be Flexible

Each of your goals must be accommodating to whatever life brings your way. Situations change, people change, and desires and wants all change family goals. Be prepared to be flexible with however the state of your family affairs changes your course.

Every pilot expects that course corrections (changes in wind direction and velocity, inclement weather, payload, etc.) will be necessary during flight. Within the family unit, changes that affect goals and plans might include changes in health, family size or incomes.

When Setting Financial Goals, Begin With the First Step

Start now. Right now. Ask questions, do research and consult a professional. Get the advice and information that you need to create a plan today. It is important to think it all through. It's important to blueprint your strategic plan. It's also important to see the eventual result.

One does not always know all of the forks in the road when beginning the journey. But if you know where you are now and where you want to be, then you can start with that knowledge and get moving to where you want to end up. You probably already have some ideas about just what kind of goals would be of interest to your family members. By setting goals, you have a direction to head in.

The best way to get started is to just start! Don't get caught up in the little things and miss the big picture! By never getting started, you are being defeated by time. If you move ahead and do not get bogged down with the daily problems and challenges of life, you can make time your friend. Time is either your greatest asset or your worst enemy.

Principle 7

The Principle of Investing For Your Future

"Steady plodding brings prosperity; hasty speculation brings poverty."

Proverbs 21:5 [TLB]

Living for the Moment

Some people seem to live only for the moment. They figure that, when they get old, someone will have to take care of them. Besides, they want to have fun now and enjoy life. They think that saving and investing will cramp their lifestyle. Well certainly it will cut back on the amount of cash flow available for fun things, but if a person will save just 10 percent of their current disposable income for retirement after taxes and tithing, they will still have 90 percent left for today.

An inability to live comfortably on 90 percent of your disposable income now means there is a problem with overspending. Saving and spending are not conflicting goals. Saving is merely not spending today so you can spend more tomorrow. And if you don't die young, you'll have plenty of time to savor the fruits of your frugality later on in retirement years.

Everyone needs a clearer vision of their retirement needs and the peace of mind that comes with knowing they are initiating an investment plan. Certainly, you should do a lot of reading from a variety of sources before making any kind of life-changing decisions. A person needs to read and become familiar with their personal retirement needs as well as pinpoint their goals and identify investment strategies.

This information is not designed to take the place of a tax advisor or financial planner, but is simply a means to help you begin thinking about how to approach the basic planning process.

How Much Will I Need?

The basic rule of thumb used by many financial planners is that a person will need about 60 to 90 percent of their final income before retirement to maintain their lifestyle during the non-working years. Of course, this rule will vary with everyone's situation. But the best way to address this issue of expenses during retirement is to sit down and plan a budget.

To identify future expenses there are some key questions to consider. How much traveling do you want to do in retirement? Will your medical expenses and insurance costs increase once you leave your company? Will your mortgage expense change because you plan to sell your house and relocate?

After considering the kind of retirement expenses you will be faced with, consider next the income needed to cover these expenses. In doing so, be sure to consider inflation as a factor in your retirement planning. Living expenses are likely to be greater in the future because inflation increases the cost of goods and services. It will require more dollars in the future to enjoy the comparable lifestyle you have today.

Failing to Plan

No one actively plans to fail in providing for a comfortable old age. They simply fail to plan. Our grandparents faced different problems with money than we do. They were frightened by bank failures and the depression and tended to put their money into just three places—a home, a bank and insurance. Today, we have to be prepared for the havoc that inflation can play on our investments over the long term, as well as corporate fraud or an up-and-down economy.

Pay Yourself First

After taking care of your tithing and tax obligations, the next person in line to be paid is you. Although this seems very hard to do with all of our other obligations, just get started by forming a regular habit. It will get easier as you progress.

Use direct deposit for automatic savings. It can be much easier to save when the money goes directly into a savings account. In that way, the decision to save is out of your hands. What you don't see, you are not likely to miss as much.

Start with 5 to 10 percent of every paycheck. It's easiest if your employer deducts it from your pay because you don't miss money you don't see. You could also ask your bank to move it from checking to savings every month or make automatic investments into a no-load (no sales charge) mutual fund.

Saving is more certain when someone else arranges it for you. The goal may be college for the kids. It may be retirement in a few years. It could be a new car, a boat or a summer place. A real key here is that it forces you to think ahead, beyond the next paycheck. Any successful business is one that plans for the future - many times, 5 and 10 years ahead.

Saving for Emergencies

Before we get started down the road of investing and retirement, we need to first be sure that we have set aside some funds for the unanticipated and unexpected. We do not want any financial surprises.

Earmark some money to put away for emergencies. You can call it saving for a rainy day, but sometimes, the emergency becomes a hurricane with genuine gale winds. We've stressed before how crucial it is to have a rainy-day fund: 3 to 6 months' living expenses put away in safe, liquid cash investments, in case you're unable to work. It may be due to a layoff, a health problem, a vehicle or appliance that stops working, or even a sudden death.

Yet a lot of people out there have absolutely no money saved. None. This is a very dangerous position to be in, and it puts your family at great risk.

What is the emergency fund for? Emergency funds are a stash of cash that you can get your hands on when the need arises. How much money do I need to keep on hand? Where should I keep it? These two great questions often get asked.

The best way to determine how much money you need for emergency purposes is to do some planning. Some things to think about would include:

- Travel expenses to family or relatives for illness or death
- Deductibles or co-pays on medical expenses
- Automobile deductibles or temporary replacements in case of an accident
- Auto repairs, tires and other mechanical issues
- Family or friends' weddings, travel expenses and gifts involved
- Replacement of old appliances you know are on their last leg

When you plan your budget each year, generate some numbers for any of these examples that might be applicable to you. Try to keep some money available for use in an emergency. If you can't save the money from your regular paycheck, then sell some assets. You might have some stocks to sell, some collectibles, or, at the very least, have a multi-week garage or yard sale. Unload some stuff that's been taking up way too much room in your garage.

Some places to keep your emergency funds are:

- a savings account,
- bank money market deposit accounts,
- certificates of deposit or
- money market funds.

Just remember that when you have an emergency, you are going to need the cash and need it fast.

The way to get your emergency cushion where you need it — especially if you're starting at zero — is to build it automatically. Build it into your budget.

Have $100 taken out of your checking account or paycheck each month and put into a money market fund—more if you can afford it, less if that feels like too big a burden. Trust me, if you don't see the money, you won't miss it.

And what about compounding? At 6 percent a year, that $100 monthly stake will grow to $1,339.72 just in time to start year #2 of your new budget. That may not feel like a lot, but this is money you don't plan to touch unless you absolutely have to, so it will just continue to grow.

Five years down the road, you'll have $7,500. And if you can boost your monthly contributions, your emergency stake will soar even faster. (One way to do so without feeling pinched is to increase your savings by the amount of any raise you get at work.)

Begin To Invest

Saving and investing are often used interchangeably, but they are somewhat different. Saving is storing money safely—such as in a bank or money market account—for short-term needs such as upcoming expenses or emergencies. Typically, you earn a low, fixed rate of return and can withdraw your money easily.

Investing is taking a risk with a portion of your savings—such as by buying stocks or bonds—in hopes of realizing higher long-term returns. Unlike bank savings, stocks and bonds over the long term have returned enough to outpace inflation, but they also decline in value from time to time.

Be Informed About Your Investment Risk

First of all, it is necessary to understand investment risk. No get-rich scheme will ever bring you peace and security. No method of investing, no category of investing, and no investment vehicle will shorten the time needed to see a financial return. If someone insists that they have a way for you to easily make a greater than average return on any investment, hang up the phone or turn and run the other direction. With regard to your money, there will always be someone more than willing to separate you from it. Just remember that hot tips lead to burnt fingers.

If you're like many investors, you want to get the highest possible return on your investments while assuming the least amount of risk. Unfortunately, finding a comfortable balance between risk and reward can be difficult.

When planning your investment strategy, you need to determine your risk tolerance level. The amount of risk you can handle in your portfolio depends on several factors—your age, family situation, your current income and your financial goals. The amount of risk you are willing to assume can help you determine the types of investments you may include in your portfolio.

There are several types of risk that every portfolio can be exposed to. Investment gains and losses can result from such factors as economic conditions and changes in the financial markets. In building your portfolio, you should be aware of some of the categories of risk.

Liquidity Risk

Liquidity risk means not being able to liquidate an investment quickly while keeping the original investment amount intact. This can occur with investing in bonds where the bond must be held to maturity in order for you to achieve a specific interest return. It can also be a risk should you invest in a particular stock, but find that the price is down at the same time you need to get your hands on the cash invested in that specific equity. For this reason, any dollars you need to access for the purpose of educational spending or maybe the purchase of a house should never be invested in the equities market.

Inflation Risk

Inflation risk is the danger that inflation will reduce the purchasing power of your investment over time. Low-yielding investments such as savings accounts and money market funds may not earn enough to outpace rising prices.

Economic Risk

Economic risk can surface due to the fact that slow economic growth will be too weak to sustain or improve the return on a particular investment. For example, the price of shares in growth companies that require a strong economy to sustain earnings may fall during an economic slowdown. Again, as in the case of liquidity risk, you would not want to invest any dollars required for education or other short-term needs into an investment that would have a substantial economic risk attached to it.

Interest Rate Risk

Interest rate risk occurs when changes in interest rates cause the value of certain investments to decrease. For example, when interest rates rise, the market value of fixed-income securities, such as bonds, declines. Bond investors hate inflation because it erodes the value of bonds' fixed interest payments. Investors are locked into the lower rate as the market rates rise. However, this type of risk may hold less potential for major financial damage.

Market Risk

Market risk is the risk associated with market fluctuations that can depress the value of particular investments. All stocks and bonds can be affected by downturns caused by fraud, war, or calamity. Additionally, certain types of investments can experience a major downturn should there be a slowdown in a specific industry or category of investments. Factors such as political developments, market cycles, changing investor sentiments or reaction to previous excessive rises or declines can all contribute to market volatility. Higher interest rates hurt stocks because they can slow the economy, which can crimp a company's revenue. They boost corporate borrowing costs and make stocks less attractive relative to interest-paying investments.

Company Risk

If a company's stock value decreases due to financial difficulties, this creates an instant company risk. Internal factors such as inefficient production and poor management or external factors such as problems with the industry, the economy, or trade can contribute to company risk.

Specific Risk

Specific risk involves any occurrences that may affect only a particular company. For example, the death of the founder, political developments, or heavy debt can affect a particular firm adversely. Some huge companies that have been around for a very long time, even with great products and unsoiled reputations, have fallen into the wrong hands and ended up worthless due to fraud and misrepresentation.

Know How To Minimize Your Investment Risk

Risk is not something you should try to eliminate from your portfolio. However, you must manage your risk. By choosing only ultra conservative investments, you limit the potential return on your investments. Instead, minimize your risk by diversifying your portfolio and choosing investments that will bring you peace of mind as well as your desired rate of return.

You can manage your investment risk through proper diversification, also known as asset allocation. In our world of uncertainty, it makes sense to reduce your risks wherever possible. This is especially true when it comes to investing. That's what diversification does. It's a way to reduce exposure to risk without reducing your potential for return. Diversification is the spreading of your money into a variety of investments. Changes in economic conditions affect some securities differently, but the impact of any single asset category is minimized.

Through diversification, you distribute your assets among a variety of investment categories and, thus, spread your risk. Of course, your personal situation and investment goals will affect the way in which you diversify your portfolio. You need to discern your objectives based on your age, family obligations, income needs, liquidity requirements, tax considerations, and tolerance for risk.

When you're determining your asset mix, consider these four types of diversification: across asset classes, across time horizons, across industries, and among companies.

Diversification Across Types of Securities

Investing among different categories of securities such as stocks, bonds, mutual funds, U.S. Treasuries, or money market instruments allows you to reduce your portfolio's exposure to any single part of the market. This type of diversification is also known as asset allocation.

The key to asset allocation is understanding how different categories of assets react to various market changes in relation to one another. One such correlation is that, during an economic downturn, most stocks tend to perform poorly. However, a slow economy can have just the opposite effect on the bond market. Because a sluggish economic environment is usually accompanied by lower interest rates, bonds will typically rise in value during an economic downturn. Therefore, by holding some stocks and some bonds, you can lessen the effects of economic volatility on your overall portfolio.

Diversification Across Time Horizons

While investing among different asset classes is important, proper diversification requires tailoring your portfolio to your needs. Investing across varying investment time horizons is the way to build a portfolio that is suited to your objectives, without sacrificing diversification.

For example, certificates of deposit, money market funds, and Treasury bills have relatively short time horizons. Other investments, like growth stocks, have long time horizons.

Investments with short time horizons can give your portfolio an anchor of stability. However, if your portfolio is too heavily weighted in these asset classes, you take the risk of reduced return because of declining interest rates or increased inflation.

On the other hand, investments with longer time horizons can result in significant capital appreciation in your portfolio. Stocks, for example, have historically been the best performing asset class over the long term. However, stocks require a long-term orientation in order to smooth out market volatility, the ups and downs of the market. Historically, the stock market has had up to four consecutive years of a declining market. This can devastate any portfolio immediately. If your need for money occurs during that time, not only will you lose on your investment, you may even incur substantial losses. Being too heavily weighted in investments with a long time horizon can deprive your portfolio of stability, as well as safety for emergency cash reserves over the short term. The best approach is to hold some long-term and some short-term investments to reduce overall fluctuation in your portfolio.

Diversification Across Industries

You can further diversify your portfolio by investing in companies in a variety of different industries. This reduces industry risk, the risk that an entire grouping of business will under-perform the market.

By dividing your portfolio among several industries, you ensure that its performance won't depend entirely on one type of business. Volatility in one industry will have only a negligible effect on your portfolio because you've spread your risk.

Diversification Among Different Companies

Within industries, it can make sense to diversify among stocks of different companies. This reduces what professionals call credit risk.

This is the risk that any one company will experience difficulties because of factors such as poor management, a lack of market for their products or services, or the superiority of competition. It also reduces your risk should fraud and mismanagement be perpetrated by company management.

Summary

What is debt? Debt is nothing more than borrowing from your future income to buy now what you cannot afford to purchase with current income. The only problem with borrowing money is that you have to pay it back. No pressure on a household is quite like the burden of debt. The pressure to repay debt can feel like the powerful tentacles of a giant sea monster pulling you down into the suffocating deep.

If you are to be successful at staying out of debt, financially, you must “live below your means”. If you have been living above your means, you are already in serious debt with no hope of becoming debt free unless you quickly change your financial habits. If you have been living within your means, you may be debt free, but you have little or no savings or investments to carry you through your retirement. What you must begin to do is live below your means.

The only way to reach a financial goal is to work at it. The most important step in reaching that goal is to develop a plan to achieve it. That’s why it is so important to plan ahead for your retirement and your financial future. While the idea of planning ahead and building a solid financial strategy for success can sometimes be intimidating and overwhelming, once you get started, it will become easier. With a little planning and a better understanding of what your investment options are, you too can successfully manage your money and pursue your financial goals.

I believe in you. I believe that you can successfully stay out of debt!

Source Material

21 Unbreakable Laws of Success, Max Anders, Thomas Nelson, 1996
A Christian Guide to Prosperity; Fries & Taylor, California: Communications Research, 1984
A Look At Stewardship, Word Aflame Publications, 2001
American Savings Education Council (http://www.asec.org)
Anointed For Business, Ed Silvoso, Regal, 2002
Avoiding Common Financial Mistakes, Ron Blue, Navpress, 1991
Baker Encyclopedia of the Bible; Walter Elwell, Michigan: Baker Book House, 1988
Becoming The Best, Barry Popplewell, England: Gower Publishing Company Limited, 1988
Business Proverbs, Steve Marr, Fleming H. Revell, 2001
Cheapskate Monthly, Mary Hunt
Commentary on the Old Testament; Keil-Delitzsch, Michigan: Eerdmans Publishing, 1986
Crown Financial Ministries, various publications
Customers As Partners, Chip Bell, Texas: Berrett-Koehler Publishers, 1994
Cut Your Bills in Half; Pennsylvania: Rodale Press, Inc., 1989
Debt-Free Living, Larry Burkett, Dimensions, 2001
Die Broke, Stephen M. Pollan & Mark Levine, HarperBusiness, 1997
Double Your Profits, Bob Fifer, Virginia: Lincoln Hall Press, 1993
Eerdmans' Handbook to the Bible, Michigan: William B. Eerdmans Publishing Company, 1987
Eight Steps to Seven Figures, Charles B. Carlson, Double Day, 2000
Everyday Life in Bible Times; Washington DC: National Geographic Society, 1967
Financial Dominion, Norvel Hayes, Harrison House, 1986
Financial Freedom, Larry Burkett, Moody Press, 1991
Financial Freedom, Patrick Clements, VMI Publishers, 2003
Financial Peace, Dave Ramsey, Viking Press, 2003
Financial Self-Defense; Charles Givens, New York: Simon And Schuster, 1990
Flood Stage, Oral Roberts, 1981
Generous Living, Ron Blue, Zondervan, 1997
Get It All Done, Tony and Robbie Fanning, New York:Pennsylvania: Chilton Book, 1979
Getting Out of Debt, Howard Dayton, Tyndale House, 1986
Getting Out of Debt, Mary Stephenson, Fact Sheet 436, University of Maryland Cooperative Extension Service, 1988

Giving and Tithing, Larry Burkett, Moody Press, 1991
God's Plan For Giving, John MacArthur, Jr., Moody Press, 1985
God's Will is Prosperity, Gloria Copeland, Harrison House, 1978
Great People of the Bible and How They Lived; New York: Reader's Digest, 1974
How Others Can Help You Get Out of Debt; Esther M. Maddux, Circular 759-3,
How To Make A Business Plan That Works, Henderson, North Island Sound Limited, 1989
How To Manage Your Money, Larry Burkett, Moody Press, 1999
How to Personally Profit From the Laws of Success, Sterling Sill, NIFP, Inc., 1978
How to Plan for Your Retirement; New York: Corrigan & Kaufman, Longmeadow Press, 1985
Is God Your Source?, Oral Roberts, 1992
It's Not Luck, Eliyahu Goldratt, Great Barrington, MA: The North River Press, 1994
Jesus CEO, Laurie Beth Jones, Hyperion, 1995
John Avanzini Answers Your Questions About Biblical Economics, Harrison House, 1992
Living on Less and Liking It More, Maxine Hancock, Chicago, Illinois: Moody Press, 1976
Making It Happen; Charles Conn, New Jersey: Fleming H. Revell Company, 1981
Master Your Money Or It Will Master You, Arlo E. Moehlenpah, Doing Good Ministries, 1999
Master Your Money; Ron Blue, Tennessee: Thomas Nelson, Inc. 1986
Miracle of Seed Faith, Oral Roberts, 1970
Mississippi State University Extension Service
Money, Possessions, and Eternity, Randy Alcorn, Tyndale House, 2003
More Than Enough, David Ramsey, Penguin Putnam Inc, 2002
Moving the Hand of God, John Avanzini, Harrison House, 1990
Multiplication, Tommy Barnett, Creation House, 1997
NebFacts, Nebraska Cooperative Extension
New York Post
One Up On Wall Street; New York: Peter Lynch, Simon And Schuster, 1989
Personal Finances, Larry Burkett, Moody Press, 1991
Portable MBA in Finance and Accounting; Livingstone, Canada: John Wiley & Sons, Inc., 1992
Principle-Centered Leadership, Stephen R. Covey, New York: Summit Books, 1991
Principles of Financial Management, Kolb & DeMong, Texas: Business Publications, Inc., 1988
Rapid Debt Reduction Strategies, John Avanzini, HIS Publishing, 1990
Real Wealth, Wade Cook, Arizona: Regency Books, 1985
See You At The Top, Zig Ziglar, Louisianna: Pelican Publishing Company, 1977
Seed-Faith Commentary on the Holy Bible, Oral Roberts, Pinoak Publications, 1975

Sharkproof, Harvey Mackay, New York: HarperCollins Publishers, 1993
Smart Money, Ken and Daria Dolan, New York: Random House, Inc., 1988
Strong's Concordance, Tennessee: Crusade Bible Publishers, Inc.,
Success by Design, Peter Hirsch, Bethany House, 2002
Success is the Quality of your Journey, Jennifer James, New York: Newmarket Press, 1983
Swim with the Sharks Without Being Eaten Alive, Harvey Mackay, William Morrow , 1988
The Almighty and the Dollar; Jim McKeever, Oregon: Omega Publications, 1981
The Challenge, Robert Allen, New York: Simon And Schuster, 1987
The Family Financial Workbook, Larry Burkett, Moody Press, 2002
The Management Methods of Jesus, Bob Briner, Thomas Nelson, 1996
The Millionaire Next Door, Thomas Stanley & William Danko, Pocket Books, 1996
The Money Book for Kids, Nancy Burgeson, Troll Associates,1992
The Money Book for King's Kids; Harold E. Hill, New Jersey: Fleming H. Revell Company, 1984
The Seven Habits of Highly Effective People, Stephen Covey, New York: Simon And Schuster, 1989
The Wealthy Barber, David Chilton, California: Prima Publishing, 1991
Theological Wordbook of the Old Testament, Chicago, Illinois: Moody Press, 1981
Treasury of Courage and Confidence, Norman Vincent Peale, New York: Doubleday & Co., 1970
True Prosperity, Dick Iverson, Bible Temple Publishing, 1993
Trust God For Your Finances, Jack Hartman, Lamplight Publications, 1983
University of Georgia Cooperative Extension Service, 1985
Virginia Cooperative Extension
Webster's Unabridged Dictionary, Dorset & Baber, 1983
What Is an Entrepreneur; David Robinson, MA: Kogan Page Limited, 1990
Word Meanings in the New Testament, Ralph Earle, Michigan: Baker Book House, 1986
Word Pictures in the New Testament; Robertson, Michigan: Baker Book House, 1930
Word Studies in the New Testament; Vincent, New York: Charles Scribner's Sons, 1914
Worth
You Can Be Financially Free, George Fooshee, Jr., 1976, Fleming H. Revell Company.
Your Key to God's Bank, Rex Humbard, 1977
Your Money Counts, Howard, Dayton, Tyndale House, 1997
Your Money Management, MaryAnn Paynter, Circular 1271, University of Illinois Cooperative Extension Service, 1987.
Your Money Matters, Malcolm MacGregor, Bethany Fellowship, Inc., 1977
Your Road to Recovery, Oral Roberts, Oliver Nelson, 1986

Comments On Sources

Over the years I have collected bits and pieces of interesting material, written notes on sermons I've heard, jotted down comments on financial articles I've read, and gathered a lot of great information. It is unfortunate that I didn't record the sources of all of these notes in my earlier years. I gratefully extend my appreciation to the many writers, authors, teachers and pastors from whose articles and sermons I have gleaned much insight.

Rich Brott

Online Resources

American Savings Education Council (http://www.asec.org)
Bloomberg.com (http://www.bloomberg.com)
Bureau of the Public Debt Online (http://www.publicdebt.treas.gov)
BusinessWeek (http://www.businessweek.com)
Charles Schwab & Co., Inc. (http://www.schwab.com)
Consumer Federation of America (http://www.consumerfed.org)
Debt Advice.org (http://www.debtadvice.org)
Federal Reserve System (http://www.federalreserve.gov)
Fidelity Investments (http://www.fidelity.com)
Financial Planning Association (http://www.fpanet.org)
Forbes (www.forbes.com)
Fortune Magazine (http://www.fortune.com)
Generous Giving (http://www.generousgiving.org/)
Investing for Your Future (http://www.investing.rutgers.edu)
Kiplinger Magazine (http://www.kiplinger.com/)
Money Magazine (http://money.cnn.com)
MorningStar (http://www.morningstar.com)
MSN Money (http://moneycentral.msn.com)
Muriel Siebert (http://www.siebertnet.com)
National Center on Education and the Economy (http://www.ncee.org)
National Foundation for Credit Counseling (http://www.nfcc.org)
Quicken (http://www.quicken.com)
Smart Money (http://www.smartmoney.com)
Social Security Online (http://www.ssa.gov)
Standard & Poor's (http://www2.standardandpoors.com)
The Dollar Stretcher, Gary Foreman, (http://www.stretcher.com)
The Vanguard Group (http://flagship.vanguard.com)
U.S. Securities and Exchange Commission (http://www.sec.gov)
Yahoo! Finance (http://finance.yahoo.com)

Magazine Resources

Business Week
Consumer Reports
Forbes
Kiplinger's Personal Finance
Money
Smart Money
US News and World Report

Newspaper Resources

Barrons
Investors Business Daily
USA Today
Wall Street Journal
Washington Times

Additional Resources by Rich Brott

5 Simple Keys to Financial Freedom

Change Your Life Forever!

By Rich Brott

6" x 9", 108 pages
ISBN 1-60185-022-0
ISBN (EAN) 978-1-60185-022-5

Order online at:

www.amazon.com
www.barnesandnoble.com
www.booksamillion.com
www.citychristianpublishing.com
www.walmart.com

www.AbcBookPublishing.com

Additional Resources by Rich Brott

Basic Principles for Maximizing Your Personal Cash Flow

7 Steps to Financial Freedom!

By Rich Brott

6" x 9", 120 pages
ISBN 1-60185-019-0
ISBN (EAN) 978-1-60185-019-5

Order online at:

www.amazon.com
www.barnesandnoble.com
www.booksamillion.com
www.citychristianpublishing.com
www.walmart.com

www.AbcBookPublishing.com

Additional Resources by Rich Brott

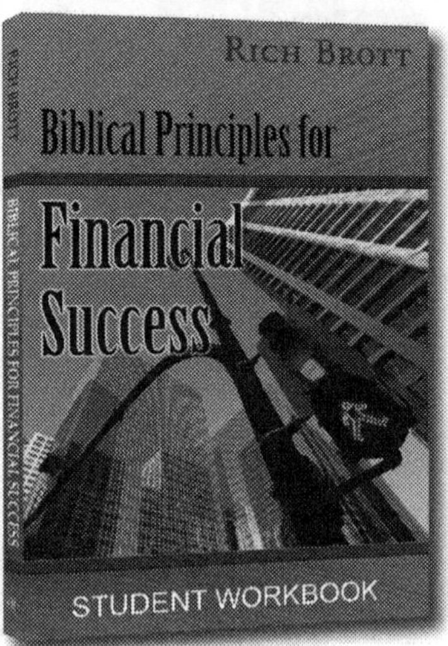

Biblical Principles for Financial Success

Student Workbook

By Rich Brott

7.5" x 9.25", 228 pages
ISBN 1-60185-016-6
ISBN (EAN) 978-1-60185-016-4

Order online at:

www.amazon.com
www.barnesandnoble.com
www.booksamillion.com
www.citychristianpublishing.com
www.walmart.com

www.AbcBookPublishing.com

Additional Resources by Rich Brott

Biblical Principles for Releasing Financial Provision!

Obtaining the Favor of God in Your Personal and Business World

By Rich Brott

7.5" x 10", 456 pages
ISBN 1-59383-021-1
ISBN (EAN) 978-1-59383-021-2

Order online at:

www.amazon.com
www.barnesandnoble.com
www.booksamillion.com
www.citychristianpublishing.com
www.walmart.com

www.AbcBookPublishing.com

www.ingramcontent.com/pod-product-compliance
Lightning Source LLC
LaVergne TN
LVHW020644100826
845148LV00012B/2325